# CADFÆL COUNTRY

*Field of chamomile and poppies, near the Wrekin*

*TO EDITH PARGETER*

**ALSO BY ROB TALBOT AND ROBIN WHITEMAN**

**THE COTSWOLDS**

**THE ENGLISH LAKES**

**SHAKESPEARE'S AVON**

A Macdonald Book

Text and photographs copyright © Talbot-Whiteman, 1990
Brother Cadfael copyright © Brother Cadfael Products Ltd, 1990
Introduction and quotes from *The Chronicles of Brother Cadfael* © Ellis Peters, 1990

First published in Great Britain in 1990
by Macdonald & Co (Publishers) Ltd
Orbit House
1 New Fetter Lane
London EC4A 1AR

A member of Maxwell Macmillan Pergamon Publishing Corporation

Designed by Rachel Foster

Maps copyright © David Cuzik, 1990
Woodcuts copyright © Oriol Bath, 1990

Front and back cover photographs copyright © Talbot–Whiteman, 1990

Photographs of Henry I with William Rufus (COT VIT AXIII), p. 26;
King Stephen with hawk (COT CLAUD DII), p. 27; and Saint Benedict (AR155), p. 38,
by permission of the British Library.

**British Library Cataloguing in Publication Data**

Whiteman, Robin, *1944-*
Cadfael country.
1. Shropshire, history
I. Title  II. Talbot, Rob, *1958-*
942.4'5

ISBN 0-356-18195-6

Typeset by Leaper & Gard Ltd
Printed and bound in Great Britain by BPCC Hazell Books Ltd
Originated by Columbia Offset Ltd

# CADFAEL COUNTRY

## SHROPSHIRE & THE WELSH BORDERS

# Rob Talbot & Robin Whiteman

Introduction by

## ELLIS PETERS

Macdonald

# Contents

# Acknowledgments

Robin Whiteman and Rob Talbot would like to thank everyone who gave their time to guide them around the properties and sites featured in this book. They particularly wish to acknowledge the generous cooperation they received from the following individuals and organisations: Barbara Morley, Regional Public Affairs Manager, The National Trust (Mercia Region); John Alwyn-Jones, Regional Public Affairs Manager, The National Trust (North Wales Region); English Heritage, (Properties in Care – Midlands); English Heritage (Properties in Care – South East); Director of Recreational Services, Lincolnshire County Council.

They are also grateful to: the Reverend Ian Ross, Vicar of the Parish of the Holy Cross, for his help and advice regarding Shrewsbury Abbey; Michael Holmes, for his comments on the chapter about the Abbey; the Reverend P J Williams and the Churchwardens of the Church of Saint Giles, Shrewsbury; the Reverend C. K. Beavan and the Churchwardens of Saint Alkmund's Church, Shrewsbury; the Redundant Churches Fund, who now care for the Church of Saint Mary, Shrewsbury; The Parish Priest, Saint Winefride's, Holywell; and the Reverend Canon John D. Beckwith and the Churchwardens of the Church of Saint Mary Magdalene, Woodstock.

In addition, thanks go to: The Earl of Powis, for permission to take photographs of Ludlow Castle; Vivian Bellamy, Borough Curator, for permission to take photographs of Shrewsbury Castle; Mr and Mrs Bromley, Shropshire Country World; Dr Jane Renfrew and the President and Fellows of Lucy Cavendish College, Cambridge, for information regarding Anglo-Saxon herbs and for permission to photograph their Anglo-Saxon herb garden; Nigel Baker and Simon Buteux, Shrewsbury Heritage Project (Birmingham University Field Archaeology Unit); Shrewsbury and Atcham Borough Council; and Shropshire County Council.

Special thanks to: Judith Dooling, for all her enthusiasm and hard work; Fielder Green Associates, for access to their research; Frank Bailey for his unfailing support; and last, but by no means least, Edith Pargeter (Ellis Peters), without whose writings, guidance, patience and warm encouragement this book would not have been possible.

*River Onny near Onibury*

# Introduction

 was born and bred in Shropshire and have never yet found any sound reason for leaving it, except perhaps for the pleasure of coming back to it again, after forays into regions otherwise delightful in themselves but no substitute for home. Or perhaps that can be extended into a further reason. What do they know of Shropshire that only Shropshire know? Travel sharpens the senses as well as broadening the mind, and gives an added savour to favourite food abstained from for a while, like Easter after Lent.

But I also have a toehold over the border, by courtesy of one Welsh grandmother, and feel the tension that Housman sensed between Wales and England, centred, logically enough, in the almost-island of Shrewsbury, frequently Welsh in its early history, frequently fought over from both sides, drawing its trade from both sides and, up to half a century ago, probably hearing as much Welsh as English in its streets and markets. By whatever name – Pengwern, Scrobbesby-rig, Shrewsbury, Salop – it has always been a regional capital to the Middle March of Wales, and no ground in the kingdom has been more tramped over by armies, coveted by chieftains, ravaged by battles, sung by poets and celebrated in epics of legend and tragedy.

This central March, both sides of the border, is my home ground, and since I have always preferred to set my writings in the places I know best and value most, it has also been the scene of most of my books, and the homeland I have handed on to Brother Cadfael, Welshman of Gwynedd, crusader, seaman and monk of Shrewsbury Abbey, a late *conversus* to the cloistered life.

Brother Cadfael arose naturally, as central figure in the first novel of the sequence, based on the actual early history of Shrewsbury's Benedictine abbey, and has survived to undertake a pilgrimage through the entire local and national history of the town and region during the anarchy of the twelfth century. There is an inherent difficulty in having a monk as protagonist in such a chronicle, since his vows included one of stability, and that meant being content to stay within the enclave itself, unless sent out on official business and at the abbot's orders, which allows his creator only a limited canvas. But the great abbeys had lands, granges, churches and fisheries, scattered fairly widely, and were committed to a certain amount of administration and management accordingly, and there were plenty of occasions for sending brothers out upon lawful business. With his modest acquired skills in medicine and the use of herbs, Cadfael enlarged his field legitimately from Lichfield and Elford in the east to Tregeiriog and Gwytherin in the west, and from Oswestry in the north to Ludlow and Clee in the south, besides his forays into the villages closer to home.

Words can convey, on occasion, very vivid visual images of place and weather and season, and landscapes familiar and well loved tend to accentuate the pictorial quality in the writing. But still there is ample room for another dimension, and the camera, in sensitive hands and with an inspired eye guiding it, can provide its own additional poetry and radiance. Place, time, weather, dawn and dark, bursting of bud and fall of leaf, bird and beast and flower, sunlight and mist and cloud, cloister and church, river and mill and field, look for them all within the covers of this book, and even after eight centuries you may find yourself, now and then, seeing the Marches very much as Cadfael saw them, perhaps thinking the same thoughts and experiencing the same contemplative pleasure that illuminated his chosen lot in life. The works and signs of man's activity have suffered more from time than have woodland and hedgerow, but even so the long continuity of human occupation is there to be seen in the worn stone of church and castle and the shaping of field and village; and the unbroken thread of life and worship persists in the very soil, and reminds us that we are the custodians of this earth, the inheritors of its history and the trustees of its future.

It is my hope that Robin Whiteman's meticulous text and Rob Talbot's beautiful photographs may give you as much pleasure as, in preparation, they have already given me. And that even after another eight centuries our descendants will still find indestructible beauty and awe and wonder in Cadfael Country.

*Ellis Peters.*

*Shrewsbury Abbey from the south*

# Brother Cadfael

he heat of the sun rebounded from honed facets of pale, baked rock, scorching his face, as the floating arid dust burned his throat. From where he crouched with his fellows in cover he could see the long crest of the wall, and the steel-capped heads of the guards on the turrets glittering in the fierce light. A landscape carved out of reddish stone and fire, all deep gullies and sheer cliffs, with never a cool green leaf to temper it, and before him the object of all his journeyings, the holy city of Jerusalem, crowned with towers and domes within white walls. The dust of battle hung in the air, dimming the clarity of battlement and gate, and the hoarse shouting and clashing of armour filled his ears. He was waiting for the trumpet to sound the final assault, and keeping well in cover while he waited, for he had learned to respect the range of the short, curly Saracen bow. He saw the banners surge forward out of hiding, streaming on the burning wind. He saw the flash of the raised trumpet, and braced himself for the blare.

The sound that brought him leaping wide-awake out of his dream was loud enough and stirring enough, but not the brazen blast of a trumpet, nor was he launched from his stillness towards the triumphant storming of Jerusalem. He was back in his stall in the dark corner of the chapter-house.

It was Brother Cadfael's habit to doze during the dull, routine businesses of the house, confident, since 'he held no troublesome parchment office', that it was unlikely he would be called upon to speak. One of his conscious decisions, shortly after entering the Rule of Saint Benedict in the Abbey of Saint Peter and Saint Paul, at Shrewsbury, was to select a seat in the chapter-house, 'well to the rear and poorly lit, half-concealed behind one of the stone pillars'. During his crusading and seafaring past, Cadfael had acquired the knack of sleeping 'without quite sleeping', which he had put to good use since he took the cowl.

Sitting 'bolt upright and undetected in his shadowy corner' of the chapter-house, he had a 'sixth sense which alerted him at need, and brought him awake instantly and plausibly. He had even been known to answer a question pat, when it was certain he had been asleep when it was put to him.'

Cadfael ap Meilyr ap Dafydd 'sprang to life suddenly and unexpectedly when he was approaching sixty, mature, experienced, fully armed and seventeen years tonsured', wrote his creator, Ellis Peters, in the introduction to *A Rare Benedictine*. 'His name,' she confides, 'was chosen as being so rare that I can find it only once in Welsh history, and even in that instance it disappears almost as soon as it is bestowed in baptism. Saint Cadog, contemporary and rival of Saint David, a powerful saint in Glamorgan, was actually christened Cadfael, but ever after seems to have been "familiarly known", as Sir John Lloyd says, as Cadog. A name of which the saint had no further need, and which appears, as far as I know, nowhere else, seemed just the thing for my man.' However, she warns wryly: 'No implication of saintliness was intended.'

Ellis Peters' medieval protagonist was 'launched on the world' as a 'squat, barrel-chested, bandy-legged veteran of fifty-seven', with a 'rolling, seaman's gait' and 'two broad feet' that had always been firmly planted on the ground. 'Solid and practical', 'without personal ambitions', Cadfael had been a Benedictine monk of Shrewsbury for nearly seventeen years, 'with a world of experience stored away inside him, and still as tough as a badger'. Although he was 'somewhat over the peak of a man's prime' and beginning to feel his years in small ways – the occasional rheumatic creak in his joints and twinge in his back – Cadfael had 'a nose sharp as fox or hound', 'the hearing of a wild creature' and eyesight that was excellent for his age. Short, sturdy, 'below middle height', with a 'broad, weathered face', he had a 'blunt, battered and brown nose', 'bushy eyebrows' and a thick hedge of bushy, greying hair ringing his nut-brown tonsure. His complexion was of 'a rosy russet colouring, confirmed by long years of outdoor living in both east and west, so engrained now that winters merely tarnished it a little, and summers regularly renewed the gloss'.

'Cadfael's warrior blood, long since abjured, had a way of coming to the boil when he heard steel in the offing. His chief uneasiness was that he could not be truly penitent about it. His king was not of this world, but in this world he could not help having a preference.' And that preference was for King Stephen, probably because he had briefly met 'and liked the man, even at his ill-advised worst, when he had slaughtered the garrison of Shrewsbury Castle'.

If Cadfael had to confess to a prevalent sin, it was to being 'endlessly curious' – a sin which, he admitted, was 'well worth a penance'. 'As long as man is curious about his fellow man,' he said, 'that appetite alone will keep him alive.' But, of all his vows, it was the vow of obedience that he always found the hardest to keep.

*The north porch,
Shrewsbury Abbey*

*Choir and parish altar,*
*Shrewsbury Abbey*

*'All the shapes within the vast stone ship showed dimly by the small altar lamps. Cadfael never passed through without stepping for a moment into the choir, to cast a glance and a thought towards Saint Winifred's altar, in affectionate remembrance of their first encounter, and gratitude for her forbearance.'*

*An Excellent Mystery*

To enable Cadfael to be in a position to solve the complex murders and mysteries that occur inside and outside the walls of Shrewsbury Abbey, it was essential for him to be able to have a reason to escape from the confines of the cloister; not just once, but regularly. Ellis Peters' inspired solution was to make him a herbalist who, in order to be able to doctor the sick, 'had, within reason, authority to come and go as he thought fit, even to absent himself from services if his aid was required elsewhere'. Through the continual process of going in and out of 'a workshop saturated with years of harvesting herbs', Cadfael could not help but 'carry the scent of them about his garments'.

In the *Eighth Chronicle of Brother Cadfael* (*The Devil's Novice*), when asked what he did in the monastery, Cadfael replied: 'I grow herbs, and dry them, and make remedies for all the ills that visit us. I physic a great many souls besides those of us within.' Pressed further, on whether his chosen vocation satisfied him, he said: 'To heal men, after years of injuring them? What could be more fitting? A man does what he must do, whether the duty he has taken on himself is to fight, or to salvage poor souls from the fighting, to kill, to die or to heal.' Cadfael had learned much of his craft in the Holy Land from both Saracen and Syrian physicians and, without any formal training, had acquired his medical skills 'by experience, by trial and study, accumulating knowledge over the years, until some preferred his ministrations to those of the acknowledged physicians'.

 *'The vegetable gardens of the Gaye unfolded green and neat along the riverside, the uncut grass of the bank making a thick emerald barrier between water and tillage. Beyond were the orchards, and then two fields of grain and the disused mill, and after that trees and bushes leaning over the swift, silent currents, crowding an overhanging bank, indented here and there by little coves, where the water lay deceptively innocent and still, lipping sandy shallows. Cadfael wanted comfrey and marsh mallow, both the leaves and the roots, and knew exactly where they grew profusely.'*
The Heretic's Apprentice

ABOVE: *Marsh mallow (marsh marigold)*; BELOW: *Lovage*

*Plants and herbs have been used since ancient times for a whole range of purposes, including cooking, dyeing and making medicine, perfumes and insecticides. The Anglo-Saxon herb garden at Lucy Cavendish College, Cambridge, was established in 1987 to show the range of plants known to have been used in Anglo-Saxon England. Evidence that the herbs now grown in the garden were used over a thousand years ago has been painstakingly gathered from two main areas of investigation: the physical remains of plants, mainly seeds, discovered during archaeological excavations; and literary references, especially medical books from monastic libraries, successive copies of which were sometimes beautifully illustrated.*

Cadfael made his debut in *A Morbid Taste for Bones*, first published in 1977, a chronicle based on Prior Robert Pennant's historical expedition into Wales in 1137 to bring back the bones of Saint Winifred for Shrewsbury Abbey. This fictional monk, herbalist and medieval detective, 'coming, as he did, of antique Welsh stock without superhuman pretensions', was born fourteen years after the Norman Conquest in the year 1080 in the vale of Conway, 'near by Trefriw' (Gwynedd). 'Cadfael's numerous kinsfolk, first and second cousins and shared forbears' ranged across North Wales 'over much of Clywd and part of Gwynedd'.

'Bred up on the borders with a foot on either side', Cadfael came to Shrewsbury with the household of an English wool-merchant. As he recalled:

> Fourteen, I was then – in Wales fourteen is manhood, and as I was a good lad with the short bow, and took kindly to the sword, I suppose I was worth my keep. The best of my following years were spent in Shrewsbury; I know it like my own palm, abbey and all. My master sent me there a year and more, to get my letters. But I quit that service when he died. I'd pledged nothing to his son, and he was a poor shadow of his father.

Shortly after, in a fit of youthful enthusiasm, he took up the Cross and left England for the Holy Land, leaving behind him a young girl of seventeen, Richildis, to whom he had been 'affianced, though nobody knew it but themselves, and probably her family would have made short work of the agreement if they had known of it'.

Having vowed to return to Shrewsbury to 'claim' her, Cadfael had 'forgotten everything in the fever and glamour and peril of a life divided impartially between soldier and sailor, and delayed his coming far too long; and she, for all her pledges to wait for him, had tired at last and succumbed to her parent's urgings, and married a more stable character'.

For fifteen years Cadfael roved as far afield as Venice, Cyprus and the Holy Land, fighting in one campaign after another, first as a soldier and later as a sailor. In 1098, he was in the First Crusade 'with Godfrey de Bouillon at Antioch, when the Saracens surrendered it'. The following year he was at the seige and storming of Jerusalem, in which, it is estimated, 70,000 Muslims were massacred. In August of the same year he was 'at the fight at Ascalon', when he came up against 'the Fatamids of Egypt'. And 'when the king of Jerusalem ruled all the coast of the Holy Land', he took to the seas and 'spent ten years as a sea captain about the coasts of the Holy Land, where fighting hardly ceased'.

There were women also 'with whom he had enjoyed encounters pleasurable to both parties, and no harm to either': 'Arianna, the Greek boat-girl'; Bianca, whom he met in Venice; and Mariam, 'the Saracen widow who sold spices and fruits in Antioch, and found him man enough to replace for a while the man she had lost'.

*Welsh Mountains from Carreg-y-Ffordd, Conwy Valley, Gwynedd*

It was at Antioch that Cadfael 'began and ended his long career as a crusader, and his love affair with Palestine, that lovely inhospitable, cruel land of gold and sand and drought'. He had first met Mariam there, selling her 'fruit and vegetables in the Street of the Sailmakers, her young, fine-boned face honed into gold and silver by the fierce sunlight, her black, oiled hair gleaming beneath her veil. She had graced his arrival in the east, a mere boy of eighteen, and his departure, a seasoned soldier and seafarer of thirty-three. A widow, young, passionate and lonely, a woman of the people, not to everyone's taste, too spare, too strong, too scornful. The void left by her dead man had ached unbearably, and she had drawn in the young stranger heart and soul into her life, to fill the gap. For a whole year he had known her, before the forces of the Cross had moved on to invest Jerusalem.'

In his fifty-ninth year, having been a Benedictine monk of Shrewsbury for nearly twenty years, Cadfael had good cause to remember Mariam again. In the *Sixth Chronicle (The Virgin in the Ice)*, he discovered, to his surprise and joy, that in 1113 – when he had left Antioch for the last time – Mariam was pregnant and, in due course of time, she had borne him a son.

*River Conwy near Gwydir Castle, Gwynedd*

Rising in the Cambrian Mountains at Llyn Conwy, a lake over 1,600 feet above sea level and five miles west of the mining town of Blaenau Ffestiniog, the River Conwy flows south to Pont a Conwy, plunges over a waterfall and heads north-east towards the village of Pentrefoelas. One mile before reaching the village, the Conwy veers sharply north-west and heads for the popular tourist centre of Betws-y-Coed, where there is a celebrated collection of bridges. Upstream from Betws-y-Coed, near the spectacular Conwy Falls, the river is joined by the River Machno; within a mile of their confluence, the waters of the Conwy are swelled further by the River Lledr and, beyond Betws-y-Coed, by the River Llugwy. At the small market town of Llanrwst, just outside the eastern border of Snowdonia National Park, the Conwy passes Gwydir Castle, a Tudor mansion set in attractive grounds. The three-arched bridge (Pont Fawr) over the river, built in 1636, is reputed to have been designed by Inigo Jones.

From Llanrwst the river flows north past Trefriw and, after a journey of about ten miles, enters the sea at Conwy, a fortified town with a castle built by Edward I in 1283–87.

It appears that in about 1114 Cadfael returned briefly to England to discover that Richildis had tired of waiting for him and married 'an honest craftsman of Shrewsbury'. Shortly after he enlisted in the 'muddled mêlée of a war' in which the English under Henry I fought to consolidate their earlier conquest of Normandy. Although Henry's brother, Robert of Normandy, was defeated and imprisoned for life in 1106, fighting continued sporadically for another thirteen or so years, until the King had 'got everything he wanted, married his son to Anjou and Maine, and made an end of fighting'.

The account of Cadfael's decision to abandon arms for the cowl is told in *A Light on the Road to Woodstock (A Rare Benedictine)*. He is not a convert, however, 'for this is not a conversion', as Ellis Peters emphasises in her introduction.

In an age of relatively uncomplicated faith, not yet obsessed and tormented by cantankerous schisms, sects and politicians, Cadfael has always been an unquestioning believer. What happens to him on the road to Woodstock is simply the acceptance of a revelation from within that the life he has lived to date, active, mobile and often violent, has reached its natural end, and he is confronted by a new need and a different challenge.

*Vale of Conwy from Llanrwst, Gwynedd*

Cadfael sailed into Southampton from Normandy in mid-November 1120, in the employ of Roger Mauduit, a Northampton knight who owned a manor at Sutton Mauduit. He had agreed to remain in his service, as man-at-arms, until 'a certain lawsuit' Roger had against the Abbey of Shrewsbury was resolved. King Henry had intended to preside over the case himself at Woodstock, near Oxford, on 23 November. But, after the tragic news that the *Blanche Nef* (White Ship) had sunk crossing the Channel, drowning his son and heir, Prince William, Henry 'willed that his justice should still prevail' and delegated the judgement to his officers.

Prior Heribert (later to become Abbot) was kidnapped by Roger Mauduit's men to prevent him from bringing the abbey's case before the King's court. Due to Cadfael's intervention, however, the prior escaped and, free to attend and present his evidence, received judgement in the abbey's favour. With the conclusion of Roger's suit, Cadfael was released from his service.

Still carrying his weapons, he immediately went to Vespers in the parish church at Woodstock, 'for no better reason – or so he thought then – than that the dimness within the open doorway beckoned him as he turned his back on a duty completed, inviting him to quietness and thought, and the bell was just sounding. The little prior was there, ardent in thanksgiving, one more creature who had fumbled his way to the completion of a task, and the turning of a leaf in the book of his life.'

> Cadfael watched out the office, and stood mute and still for some time after priest and worshippers had departed. The silence after their going was deeper than the ocean and more secure than the earth. Cadfael breathed and consumed it like new bread. It was the light touch of a small hand on the hilt of his sword that startled him out of that profound isolation. He looked down to see a little acolyte, no higher than his elbow, regarding him gravely from great round eyes of blinding blue, intent and challenging, as solemn as ever was angelic messenger.
>
> 'Sir,' said the child in stern treble reproof, tapping the hilt with an infant finger, 'should not all weapons of war be laid aside here?'
>
> 'Sir,' said Cadfael hardly less gravely, though he was smiling, 'you may very well be right.' And slowly he unbuckled the sword from his belt, and went and laid it down, flatlings, on the lowest step under the altar. It looked strangely appropriate and at peace there. The hilt, after all, was a cross.

Later that same day, Cadfael went to seek an audience with Prior Heribert, who was returning to Shrewsbury the next morning. 'The little man came out graciously to welcome a stranger, and knew him for an acquaintance at least, and now at a breath certainly a friend.

'"Father," Cadfael said simply, "here am I at the turning of my life, free of one man's service, and finished with arms. Take me with you!"'

*Church of St Mary
Magdalene, Woodstock,
Oxfordshire*

*Norman south door, Church of St Mary Magdalene, Woodstock, Oxfordshire*

*Founded in the reign of Henry II (1153–1189) as a chapel-of-ease to the Parish Church of St Martin at the nearby village of Bladon, the Church of St Mary Magdalene was often used by the King when he was in residence at his royal manor of Woodstock. The only surviving feature of the original church is the Norman south door decorated with a zig-zag pattern which, dispensing with the usual capitals, goes round the arch and down both sides to the ground. Over the centuries the church was altered and enlarged and in 1878 it was extensively restored. Preserved inside the church, on the south arcade, are over twenty beautifully carved stone heads thought to be portraits of people living in the thirteenth century, including a man wearing a coronet said to be King Henry III (1216–1272).*

Having lived most of his life 'in the thick of battles', Cadfael returned with the Benedictine brothers of the Abbey of Saint Peter and Saint Paul at Shrewsbury in November 1120 to become a monk. Despite the fact that he had come late to monastic life, 'like a battered ship settling at last for a quiet harbour', he never had any regrets. Gradually, over the years, he worked hard to create one of the finest Benedictine herb gardens in the whole of England, stocked with 'many exotic plants of his own careful raising', collected in his travels throughout Europe and the Holy Land. It was 'his own small kingdom' and within it 'he ruled unchallenged'. In a sheltered corner of the walled herbarium he had a wooden work-shed, 'his own particular pride', where he prepared his medicines, dried his herbs and brewed his mysteries. It was 'a home within a home'; a refuge within which he could withdraw from the outside world, 'always a convenient excuse for not being where according to the horarium he should have been'; and a place where he 'spent so much of his time, and did his best thinking'.

> He was well aware that in the first years of his vows the novices and lay servants had been wont to point out to one another with awed whisperings,
>
> 'See that brother working in the garden there? The thickset fellow who rolls from one leg to the other like a sailor? You wouldn't think to look at him, would you, that he went on crusade when he was young? ... Hard to believe it now, eh?'
>
> Brother Cadfael himself found nothing strange in his wide-ranging career, and had forgotten nothing and regretted nothing. He saw no contradiction in the delight he had taken in battle and adventure, and the keen pleasure he now found in quietude. Spiced, to be truthful, with more than a little mischief when he could get it, as he liked his victuals well flavoured, but quietude all the same, a ship becalmed and enjoying it.

Whenever his friend Hugh Beringar, the Sheriff of Shropshire, came to the abbey to confer with the Abbot on 'shire affairs' he always sought Cadfael out afterwards and, more often than not, found him working in his herb garden or busy in his workshop. Together they spent many pleasurable hours 'sitting easy', sharing a jug of wine and chatting beneath the 'rustling bunches of dried herbs hung from the roof-beams'.

And sometimes, when he was alone and had nothing more to do than put his feet up on the wooden bench, Cadfael 'remembered and acknowledged with gratitude and joy the years of his sojourning in the world, the lusty childhood and venturous youth, the taking of the Cross and the passion of the Crusade, the women he had known and loved, the years of his sea-faring off the coast of the Holy Kingdom of Jerusalem, all that pilgrimage that had led him here at last to his chosen retreat. None of it wasted, however foolish and amiss, nothing lost, nothing vain, all of it somehow fitting him to the narrow niche where he now served and rested.'

Yes, indeed, Brother Cadfael 'had no need to regret anything'. And what he 'did not regret, he found grave difficulty in remembering to confess'.

*Shrewsbury Castle*

# King Stephen and the Empress Maud

I n the year 1100 – on the death of his brother, William Rufus – Henry, the youngest son of William the Conqueror, seized the crown of England. Rufus was killed by an arrow while hunting in the New Forest and, despite later speculation that Henry might have 'arranged' his brother's death, it was widely held to have been an accident. Robert of Normandy, the eldest of the Conqueror's three sons and rightful heir to the English throne, was in Jerusalem at the time. The *Chronicles of Brother Cadfael* state that Cadfael had been a part of Robert's 'mongrel' company during the First Crusade and, when Jerusalem 'was settled and Baldwin crowned', had taken to the sea and become a sailor.

Although Robert returned to Normandy in September 1100, it was not until the following year that he attempted an invasion. When he landed with a considerable force at Portsmouth in July 1101, many of the great Norman barons in England rallied to his side, including the powerful Earl Robert de Bellême, the son of Earl Roger de Montgomery, founder of Shrewsbury Abbey (see Shrewsbury Abbey, p. 69).

The two armies met at Alton, near Winchester. But instead of resolving their dispute on the field of battle, both sides withdrew to explore the possibility of a peaceful settlement. In the event, a treaty was successfully negotiated, allowing Henry to keep the crown of England in return for paying his brother, Robert of Normandy, a pension of 2,000 pounds a year. Henry also agreed to renounce any claims to lands in Normandy, excepting the fortress of Domfront.

*Henry I with his brother
William Rufus*

Once the danger was over, however, and Robert had returned to Normandy, Henry set about strengthening his realm by removing any further threat of either rebellion or invasion. One by one he confiscated the lands of the prominent Normans who had opposed him, including the powerful Robert de Bellême, who was banished from the kingdom, having forfeited his earldom and had his strongholds in the Welsh Marches seized.

But Henry was not content just to assert his royal authority; he was also set on taking Normandy from his brother. In 1106, at the battle of Tinchebrai, Robert was captured and imprisoned for the remaining twenty-eight years of his life. With the incarceration of his brother, Henry had removed the main threat to his authority and power, yet the wars in Normandy dragged on intermittently for years.

In November 1120 Cadfael, 'experienced and accomplished in arms', sailed from Normandy to England in the service of Roger Mauduit, a Northampton knight. Although he was unaware of it at the time, the Welsh man-at-arms was at the turning of his life, for before the year was out he was to exchange the discipline of a soldier for that of a monk.

Henry I was in Normandy when Cadfael crossed the Channel for the last time. *A Light on the Road to Woodstock (A Rare Benedictine)* sets the scene:

> The King's court was in no hurry to return to England, that late autumn of 1120, even though the fighting, somewhat desultory in these last stages, was long over, and the enforced peace sealed by a royal marriage. King Henry had brought to a successful conclusion his sixteen years of patient, cunning, relentless plotting, fighting and manipulating, and could now sit back in high content, master not only of England but of Normandy, too. What the Conqueror had misguidedly dealt out in two separate parcels to his elder sons, his youngest son had now put together again and clamped into one. Not without a hand in removing from the light of day, some said, both of his brothers, one of whom had been shovelled into a hasty grave under the tower at Winchester, while the other was now a prisoner in Devizes, and unlikely ever to be seen again by the outer world.
>
> The court could well afford to linger to enjoy victory, while Henry trimmed into neatness the last loose edges still to be made secure. But his fleet was already preparing at Barfleur for the voyage back to England, and he would be home before the month ended.

In that autumn of 1120, having finally triumphed over French and Angevin opposition to become master of England and Normandy, Henry suffered a dreadful tragedy that upset everything he had planned. On the night of 25 November, the *Blanche Nef* (White Ship), in which his only legitimate son and heir, Prince William, 'with all his companions and many other noble souls were embarked, put to sea late, and was caught in gales before ever clearing Barfleur.

The ship was lost, split upon a rock, foundered with all hands', and 'half the young chivalry of England' was 'wiped out in one blow'.

> So that was the end of one man's year of triumph, an empty achievement, a ruinous victory, Normandy won, his enemies routed, and now everything swept aside, broken apart upon an obstinate rock, washed away in a malicious sea. His only lawful son, recently married in splendour, now denied even a coffin and a grave, for if ever they found those royal bodies it would be by the relenting grace of God, for the sea seldom put its winnings ashore by Barfleur. Even some of his unlawful sons, of whom there were many, gone down with their royal brother, no one left but the one legal daughter to inherit a barren empire.

Henry's 'one legal daughter' was Matilda, or Maud, who was 'married in childhood to the Holy Roman Emperor Henry V' of Germany. When the Emperor died in 1125, Henry recalled the Empress Maud to England and made his barons acknowledge her as his heir. Three years later, in order to form an alliance with Fulk V of Anjou, Henry forced her to marry the count's fourteen-year-old son and heir, Geoffrey Plantagenet, or Geoffrey of Anjou.

'Countess of Anjou', according to the *Twelfth Chronicle (The Raven in the Foregate)*, was a title she 'detested, as belittling both her birth and her rank by her first marriage, a king's daughter and the widow of an emperor, now reduced to a title borrowed from her none-too-loved and none-too-loving second husband, Geoffrey of Anjou, her inferior in every particular but talent, common sense and efficiency'. In fact, it was said, all he ever did for Maud was give her three sons, one of whom she eventually saw crowned as Henry II.

When Henry I died on 1 December 1135, the Empress Maud and Geoffrey of Anjou, to whom he had promised the succession of his Anglo-Norman realm, were 'far away in Normandy, thinking no evil'. His favourite nephew, Count Stephen of Blois, however, who was little more than a day away in Boulogne, rushed to England and, with the help of his brother, Henry of Blois, Bishop of Winchester, seized the throne and had himself crowned King at Westminster within the month. Many of the barons who had sworn fealty to the Empress retracted their oaths and declared themselves for him. Stephen's action was to herald the start of a long civil war for the crown of England, a struggle, fought between cousins and rival claimants to the throne, that was to last for nearly nineteen years. It is during this troubled period – with fortune swinging like a pendulum many times between the warring factions – that the *Chronicles* are set.

The *Second Chronicle (One Corpse too Many)* is based on King Stephen's siege of Shrewsbury Castle in the summer of 1138, the year after Prior Robert Pennant's expedition into Wales to bring back the bones of Saint Winifred (see Saint Winifred, p. 85). The Sheriff, William FitzAlan, owed his office to Stephen, yet he held the castle for the Empress Maud.

*King Stephen, nephew of Henry I*

*The west front of Winchester
Cathedral, Hampshire*

*The first cathedral at Winchester, known as the Old Minster, was built by the Saxon King Cenwalh in about 645 and dedicated to St Peter. Its foundations lie just to the north of the present cathedral. The first Norman Bishop of Winchester was William Walkelin and he began the construction of the present cathedral in 1079. It was consecrated in 1093 and, shortly after, the Old Minster was demolished. Winchester Cathedral, 556 feet from east to west, is the longest in Europe. The Perpendicular arches and vaulting of the nave are the work of the fourteenth-century Bishop, William of Wykeham, who continued the transformation from Norman to Gothic started by his predecessor William of Edington. Inside the cathedral there are a number of monuments to Saxon kings and queens, the tomb of the Norman King, William Rufus, who reigned from 1087–1100, and also the graves of Jane Austen (1775–1817) and Izaak Walton (1593–1683).*

In his siege camp, deployed across the entire land approach to the Castle Foregate, between broad coils of the River Severn, King Stephen fretted, fumed and feasted, celebrating the few loyal Salopians – loyal to him, that is! – who came to offer him aid, and planning his revenge upon the many disloyal who absented themselves.

He was a big, noisy, handsome, simple-minded man, very fair in colouring, very comely in countenance, and at this stage in his fortunes totally bewildered by the contention between his natural good nature and his smarting sense of injury. He was said to be slow-witted, but when his Uncle Henry had died and left no heir but a daughter, and she handicapped by an Angevin husband and far away in France, no matter how slavishly her father's vassals had bowed to his will and accepted her as queen, Stephen for once in his life had moved with admirable speed and precision, and surprised his potential subjects into accepting him at his own valuation before they even had time to consider their own interests, much less remember reluctant vows. So why had such a successful coup abruptly turned sour? He would never understand. Why had half of his more influential subjects, apparently stunned into immobility for a time, revived into revolt now? Conscience? Dislike of the King imposed upon them? Superstitious dread of King Henry and his influence with God?

Forced to take the opposition seriously and resort to arms, Stephen had opened in the way that came naturally to him, striking hard where he must, but holding the door cheerfully open for penitents to come in. And what had been the result? He had spared, and they had taken advantage and despised him for it. He had invited submission without penalty, as he moved north against rebel holds, and the local baronage had held off from him with contempt. Well, tomorrow's dawn should settle the fate of the Shrewsbury garrison, and make an example once for all. If these midlanders would not come peacefully and loyally at his invitation, they should come scurrying like rats to save their own skins.

The following day, after a siege that had lasted four weeks, Stephen's army took Shrewsbury Castle:

> Long before noon it was all over, the gates fired with brushwood and battered down, the baileys cleared one by one, the last defiant bowman hunted down from the wall and towers, smoke heavy and thick like a pall over fortress and town. In the streets not a human creature or even a dog stirred. At the first assault every man had gone to earth with wife and family and beasts behind locked and barred doors and crouched listening with stretched ears to the thunder and clash and yelling of battle. It lasted only a short while. The garrison had reached exhaustion, ill-supplied, thinned by desertions as long as there was any possibility of escape. Everyone had been certain the next determined attack must carry the town. The merchants of Shrewsbury waited with held breath for the inevitable looting, and heaved sighs of relief when it was called to heel peremptorily by the King himself – not because he grudged his Flemings their booty but because he wanted them close about his person. Even a king is vulnerable, and this had been an enemy town, and was still unpacified. Moreover, his urgent business was with the garrison of the castle, and in particular with FitzAlan and Adeney, and Arnulf of Hesdin.

Although William FitzAlan and Fulke Adeney, loyal supporters of the Empress Maud, managed to escape, Arnulf of Hesdin was captured and, along with ninety-three others, was hanged from the walls of the castle. Stephen's chief aide, Gilbert Prestcote, 'a lean, middle-aged knight browed and nosed like a falcon, his black, forked beard veined with grey', was made Sheriff of Shropshire in place of FitzAlan. Prestcote's right-hand man, Adam Courcelle, was made his deputy. According to the *Second Chronicle*, however, Courcelle was killed shortly after during a 'trial by combat' and his victorious opponent, Hugh Beringar, was appointed deputy in his stead.

When Prestcote was murdered in 1141, Beringar became Sheriff, and throughout the rest of the *Chronicles* – despite pendulum-like swings of fortune between the two rival claimants to the throne – he doggedly remained 'King Stephen's man, and held the shire for him loyally enough, but with even greater goodwill he held it for the folk who lived in it'. Beringar 'was only too glad to be guardian of a shire which had changed hands but once', and, from the outset, was determined to 'keep King Stephen's title unchallenged and the tide of unrest at bay from its borders, whether the threat came from the Empress's forces, the unpredictable cantrips of the Welsh of Powys to the west, or the calculating ambition of the Earl of Chester in the north'. Hugh managed to balance his 'relationships with all these perilous neighbours' for many years 'with fair success'.

Hugh Beringar was 'a man whose energy did not flag as Stephen's did, who did not abandon one enterprise to go off after another, as Stephen did'. Small and slender, with a tanned, clean-shaven face and cropped black hair, his 'modest stature and light weight had deceived many a man to his undoing'. He owned a manor at Maesbury, near Oswestry, in the north-west corner of the shire, and also a house in Shrewsbury, which he shared with his wife, Aline, and their son, Giles, to whom Cadfael was godfather.

In a country debilitated by 'years of desultory civil war it behoved state and church to work closely together, and where sheriff and abbot were of like mind they could secure for their people a comparatively calm and orderly existence, and fend off the worst excesses of the times'. Hugh and Abbot Radulfus grew to know and trust each other over the years, and were 'accustomed to sharing with complete confidence, for the sake of order and England, whatever they gathered of events and tendencies, without ever questioning whether they shared the same opinions. Their disciplines were separate and very different, but their acceptance of service was one, and mutually recognised.'

Although Cadfael's first encounters with Hugh had 'been a puzzle to him', proof upon proof since then 'had sealed him friend, the closest and dearest'. Despite the difference in their ages – a gap of over thirty years – Cadfael and Hugh were 'closer than father and son, having not only that easy and tolerant relationship of two generations, but shared experiences that made of them contemporaries. They sharpened minds, one upon the other, for the better protection of values and institutions that needed defence with every passing day in a land so shaken and disrupted.'

After the siege and fall of Shrewsbury Castle, the 'tide of civil war between King Stephen and the partisans of the Empress Maud ... receded into the south-western borders, leaving Shrewsbury to recover cautiously from having backed the weaker side and paid a bloody price for it'. On 30 September 1139 the Empress Maud and her half-brother Robert of Gloucester landed near Arundel, on the south coast, and seemed to be within Stephen's grasp, but 'through the misplaced generosity of the King, or the dishonest advice of some of his false friends, had been allowed to reach Bristol, where her cause was impregnably installed already'. With both rival factions now in England the nation was in a state of anarchy.

In November 1139 the city of Worcester was taken by the forces of the Empress, and 'all those of its inhabitants who could get away in time' fled north into Shropshire. On the southern border, the castellan of Ludlow Castle, Josce de Dinan was, according to the *Sixth Chronicle (The Virgin in the Ice)*, 'contemplating defection'. It is said, though not confirmed by modern historians, that the castle was besieged in 1139 by King Stephen, who is reputed to have rescued his ally, Prince Henry of Scotland, from the hook of a grappling iron thrown down from the walls by one of the defenders.

*Ludlow Castle,
domestic buildings*

December of the following year brought news of treason in the north-east. The *Eighth Chronicle (The Devil's Novice)* relates that two days after Stephen had left Lincoln, having received pledges of loyalty from Ranulf of Chester and William of Roumare, they reneged on their oaths, 'made their way into the King's castle by a subterfuge' and took it by force. In February 1141 Stephen mustered a 'creditable force' to try and oust the Earls of Chester and Lincoln, 'ambitious half-brothers', from their hill-top fortress at Lincoln. In the battle which followed, Stephen, who bravely fought on when he might have escaped, was captured and taken to Bristol, where he was held prisoner in the castle.

The Empress Maud was up in the clouds, and Stephen, crowned and anointed though he might be, was down in the midden, close-bound and close-guarded, and his brother Henry of Blois, bishop of Winchester and papal legate, far the most influential of the magnates and hitherto his brother's supporter, had found himself in a dilemma. He could either be a hero, and adhere loudly and firmly to his allegiance, thus incurring the formidable animosity of a lady who was in the ascendant and could be dangerous, or trim his sails and accommodate himself to the reverses of fortune by coming over to her side.

He chose the latter. 'Discreetly, of course, and with well-prepared arguments to render his about face respectable.' And in the summer of 1141 the Empress was allowed to enter London and make preparations for her coronation. But 'the fool woman, with the table spread for her at Westminster and the crown all but touching her hair, had seen fit to conduct herself in so arrogant and overbearing

*The Observatory Tower at Lincoln Castle*

*Lincoln Cathedral, Lincolnshire*

*The ancient hill city of Lincoln was a settlement long before the Romans invaded England in the first century AD and built a military fortress on the limestone ridge overlooking the flat Lincolnshire plain. Strategically sited to command the meeting of two great highways, the Fosse Way and Ermine Street, Lincoln became a fortified town. By the beginning of the second century it was a colony for retired soldiers, known in its Latin form as Lindum Colonia, from which the name of Lincoln is derived.*

*In about 1072 the first Norman Bishop, Remigius, began building a great cathedral opposite the castle, on a site which dominated the town and skyline for miles around. Consecrated in 1092, it was damaged by fire in 1141 and by an earthquake in 1185. Work on rebuilding and enlarging the cathedral was started by Bishop Hugh of Avalon in 1192 and continued after his death in 1200. The spire on the central tower, rising 525 feet from the ground, collapsed in 1549 during a violent storm and the smaller spires on the two western towers were removed in 1807.*

a manner towards the citizens of London that they had risen in fury to drive her out in ignominious flight, and let King Stephen's valiant queen into the city in her place'.

A few months later, in September 1141, the Empress Maud, until then besieged in her castle at Winchester, managed to escape into the safety of her western stronghold. Robert of Gloucester, the Empress's half-brother and leader of her party, however, was captured trying to ford the River Test at Stockbridge. Maud was left with no other alternative but to exchange Stephen for Robert, 'without whom she could not hope to achieve anything. And here was England back to the beginning, with all to do again. For if she could not win, neither could she give up.'

Robert died in October 1147, and early in the following year the Empress left England disheartened, never to return. When Stephen's son and heir, Eustace, died in August 1153, a settlement was negotiated and in December, with the signing of a treaty at Westminster, it was agreed that Stephen should remain King for life and that, after his death, the Empress's son, Henry would succeed to the throne. Stephen, however, found himself King of a peaceful, undivided realm for less than a year, for on 25 October 1154 he died. He was buried beside his wife and eldest son in the small Cluniac monastery they had founded at Faversham. For the first time in over a hundred years, the next heir to the English throne was undisputed: Maud's son by Geoffrey of Anjou, with no rival contenders, was crowned King Henry II.

Wolvesey Castle,
Winchester

*To the south of Winchester Cathedral are the remains of Wolvesey Castle, a great fortified palace built in 1138 by Bishop Henry de Blois, brother of King Stephen, on the site of an earlier Anglo-Saxon bishop's palace. Bishop Henry's structure also incorporated the stone residence, now known as the West Hall, built by the Norman Bishop, William Giffard, in about 1107. In the summer of 1141, during the fratricidal war between Stephen and Maud, the Empress and her forces besieged Bishop Henry in his castle. He retaliated by setting fire to the city, and was only relieved when Maud's army, weakened by disease and starvation, decided to retreat. Wolvesey Castle was virtually abandoned in the seventeenth century and in the early 1680s Bishop George Morley decided to build a new palace in its place. The house was again neglected in the following century and in 1786 the building was demolished except for the west wing. It was used for a number of purposes until 1928, when it became once again the residence of the bishops of Winchester. The remains of the medieval palace are now in the care of English Heritage.*

Wolvesey Castle,
Winchester

*The north side of Shrewsbury Abbey showing the remains of the demolished outer walls of the north transept*

# The Benedictines

aint Benedict, the father of Western monasticism, was born in the Italian town of Nursia (present-day Norcia, some forty miles south-east of Perugia), in about AD 480. All that is known of his life, apart from what can be deduced from his Rule, is contained in the *Dialogues* of Saint Gregory the Great, who was Pope Gregory I from 590 to 604. Born into a middle-class family, Benedict was sent by his parents to Rome to be educated, but he was disgusted by the decadent culture he found there and decided to abandon his studies and devote himself to God. After staying a while in a small religious community at Enfide (modern Affile), about forty miles east of Rome, he left to become a hermit, spending several years in the solitude of the nearby mountains round Subiaco. His fame as a holy man grew and in time he was persuaded to become the Abbot of a neighbouring monastery. It is said, however, that the monks rebelled against the severity of his discipline and, after an unsuccessful attempt to poison him, he willingly returned to his solitude.

Nevertheless, his reputation for holiness was such that within a short period of time he had attracted a large number of disciples – so many, in fact, that he was able to found twelve monasteries, each containing twelve monks, with himself in overall control. Among the best known of his followers were Maurus and Placidius, both sons of Roman noblemen, who were later to travel through Gaul (roughly the territory of modern-day France, Luxembourg and Belgium) and Sicily respectively to spread the Benedictine message.

In about 529, after being at Subiaco for some thirty years, Benedict left the area, according to Saint Gregory, because of the nuisance caused by Florentius, a jealous local priest. He and a few of his disciples went to Monte Cassino, half-

*Saint Benedict, father of Western monasticism*

way between Rome and Naples, where they built a monastery on the summit of a hill overlooking Cassino. It is said that the inhabitants of the district, still mostly pagan, were converted to Christianity by his preaching. His sister, Saint Scholastica, founded a nunnery in a place called Pinmarola nearby.

In 542 Benedict was visited by Totila, King of the Goths. Rebuking Totila for his evil deeds, the Saint prophesied that he would enter Rome to rule for nine years but would die in the tenth. The prophecy was fulfilled. Saint Gregory relates many accounts of Benedict's miracle-making and prophetic abilities, including the prediction that Monte Cassino would be destroyed by 'Barbarians'. Indeed, the Lombards, one of the Germanic conquerors of Italy, sacked the monastery in 583 and it was left deserted until about 720, when it was refounded.

According to legend, Saint Benedict died on 21 March 543 at Monte Cassino, not long after the death of Saint Scholastica, and was buried there with her in the oratory of Saint John the Baptist. Although there has been a great deal of controversy about subsequent events, it seems that the remains of the two saints were removed from Italy to France in about 660, Benedict's relics ending up in the Monastery of Fleury-sur-Loire.

More than half a century after Benedict's death, Saint Augustine, the prior of Pope Gregory I's Monastery of Saint Andrew in Rome, was sent on a mission to England with some forty monks to preach the gospel. He was favourably received by Ethelbert, King of Kent, in 597 and founded a number of religious houses, including the Monastery of Saint Peter and Saint Paul outside the walls of Canterbury. In spite of some early spectacular successes, the conversion of the Anglo-Saxons was slow, with frequent relapses into paganism. Nevertheless, towards the close of the sixth century, Augustine had introduced not only Roman Christianity but also the Benedictine Order to England. From that moment onwards, the Benedictine monasteries stood unrivalled until the collective reforms of the Carthusians, Cistercians and Cluniacs, which occurred roughly in Cadfael's lifetime. The earliest order of regular canons following a monastic rule were the Augustinians, who were introduced to England in 1095. Haughmond Abbey, a house of Augustinian canons (who were also known as Black or Austin canons) was founded in about 1135 by William FitzAlan, a loyal supporter of the Empress Maud. The abbey is situated a few miles north-east of Shrewsbury and is mentioned in the *Sixteenth Chronicle of Brother Cadfael (The Heretic's Apprentice)* and the *Seventeenth Chronicle (The Potter's Field)*.

It was while he was at Monte Cassino that Saint Benedict, making extensive use of existing writings, composed the Rule for which he is famous. The document consists of a prologue and seventy-three chapters, and, according to Saint Gregory, is 'remarkable for its discretion and for the clearness of its language'. The Rule, which demanded from the monks a life-long vow of poverty, chastity, obedience and stability, was adopted not only by the Benedictines but also, with modifications, by later orders. For Brother Cadfael, the 'vow of stability, however gravely undertaken, sometimes proved as hard to keep as the vow of obedience', which he 'had always found his chief stumbling block'.

Although Saint Benedict had been a hermit, he considered that the solitary life was fraught with spiritual dangers for the young and inexperienced. His Rule, therefore, is concerned with a life spent entirely within a monastic community, with the emphasis on moderation. 'We propose', says the prologue, 'to establish a school of the Lord's service and in setting it up we hope to order nothing that is harsh or hard to bear.' The waking day was divided into three roughly equal portions to provide a balance between prayer, work and study. 'Idleness is the enemy of the soul', warns the Rule, 'and for this reason the brethren should be occupied, at fixed periods, in manual labour, and at other times in spiritual reading .

The monastic horarium differed in summer and winter because of the varying hours of daylight. The day began at midnight with Matins, the first and longest service, 'the celebration of God made flesh, virgin-born and wonderful'. This was followed, almost immediately, by Lauds, a short office which ended between one and two in the morning, after which the monks retired to their beds in the *dortoir.*

> Cadfael always rose from Matins and Lauds not sleepy and unwilling, but a degree more awake than at any other time, as though his senses quickened to the sense of separateness of the community gathered here, to a degree impossible by daylight. The dimness of the light, the solidity of the enclosing shadows, the muted voices, the absence of lay worshippers, all contributed to the sense of being enfolded in a sealed haven, where all those who shared in it were his own flesh and blood and spirit, responsible for him as he for them, even some for whom, in the active and arduous day, he could feel no love, and pretended none. The burden of his vows became also his privilege, and the night's first worship was the next day's energy.

In order to check on his workshop or to collect plants, Cadfael 'was often up well before Prime', the first office of the monastic day, which was held at dawn. Terce occurred at about nine; Sext at about noon; None at about three; Vespers in the late afternoon; and Compline, the last office before the community retired for the night, at about eight-thirty in summer and about seven-thirty in winter. The *Twelfth Chronicle (The Raven in the Foregate)* says that Cadfael went to his bed in the *dortoir,* 'mindful of the rule that the words of Compline, the completion, the perfecting of the day's worship, should be the last words uttered before sleep, that the mind should not be distracted from the "Opus Dei"'.

Immediately after Prime, at about eight-thirty in the morning, was the Morning Mass, or the Lady Mass, held for the servants and manual workers. High Mass, the principal mass of the day, was held at about ten in the morning and lasted about an hour.

Chapter, usually following the office of Prime, was held in the chapter-house, and it was here that Cadfael often dozed behind his pillar while the dull routine business of the community was being discussed. After supper in the refectory, the monks went to Collations in the chapter-house; 'the formal reading from the lives of the saints was a part of the day that Cadfael often missed if he had vulnerable preparations brewing in his workshop.' It was the tending of these culinary and medicinal preparations that always provided him with 'a convenient excuse for not being where according to the horarium he should have been'. In between these daylight offices the monks would, besides taking regular meals in the refectory, pursue the round of their duties with study and work.

The Benedictines, also known as Black monks because of the colour of their habits, not only provided for their own needs – running a self-contained and self-sufficient community – but also looked after the needs of others: teaching students; caring for the sick and the elderly; distributing alms to the poor; and housing travellers, whether penniless pilgrims or wealthy kings.

## The Officers of Shrewsbury Abbey in 1140

Saint Benedict called the abbot the father of all the monks and said, in chapter two of his Rule, that 'in the monastery he is considered to represent the person of Christ, since he is called by His name'.

In 1140 Abbot Radulfus was the head of the Abbey of Saint Peter and Saint Paul at Shrewsbury, having been 'sent from London to trim an easy-going provincial house into more zealous shape.' Like many abbots, he 'was an aristocrat and the equal of a baron', and, in addition to his monastic responsibilities, his rank meant that he was also involved in feudal and secular duties. Although Radulfus owed his office to the King and the papal legate, it was usual for the abbot to be elected by the monks and, thereafter, hold office for life. 'Though a man of few words himself', Radulfus 'was disposed, as a rule, to allow plenty of scope to those who were rambling and loquacious about their requests and suggestions'. In his fifties, he 'was more than commonly tall, erect as a lance, and sinewy, with a lean hawkface and a calmly measuring eye'. Abbot Radulfus 'had long had qualms of conscience about accepting infants committed by their fathers to the cloister, and had resolved to admit no more boys until they were of an age to make the choice for themselves'.

*The choir and nave looking towards the west window of the fourteenth-century tower, Shrewsbury Abbey*

*'In the dim space of the choir, partially shut off from the nave of the church by the parish altar, the brothers in their stalls showed like carven copies, in this twilight without age or youth, comeliness or homeliness, so many matched shadows. The height of the vault, the solid stone of the pillars and walls, took up the sound of Brother Anselm's voice, and made of it a disembodied magic, high in air.'*

*The Sanctuary Sparrow*

*The south side,*
*Shrewsbury Abbey*

*Before the Dissolution, when*
*the abbey was a Benedictine*
*monastery, the south side of the*
*church adjoined the north wall*
*of the cloister and contained no*
*windows. The present windows*
*of the south wall replaced*
*earlier ones and were inserted*
*in the early nineteenth century*

Second in command to the abbot was the prior, who had particular responsibility for maintaining order in the enclave, both spiritually and physically. In the absence of the abbot he took charge of the affairs of the monastery. Chapter sixty-five of the Rule warns that 'serious scandals often occur in monasteries because of the appointment of a prior; for there are those who, swelling up with evil pride, consider themselves to be second abbots and act like tyrants, thereby nourishing scandals and quarrels in the community'. Prior Robert Pennant, 'of mixed Welsh and English blood, was more than six feet tall, attenuated and graceful, silver-grey of hair at fifty, blanched and beautiful of visage, with long aristocratic features and lofty marble brow. There was no man in the midland shires would look more splendid in a mitre, superhuman in height and authority, and there was no man in England better aware of it, or more determined to prove it at the earliest opportunity.' Whatever 'virtues might be found in Prior Robert, humility was not one, nor magnanimity. He was invariably sure of his own rightness, and where it was challenged he was not a forgiving man.'

The prior's clerk, according to the *Chronicles*, was Brother Jerome, 'reflecting Robert's pleasure or displeasure like a small, warped mirror'. Jerome, Robert's 'ear and shadow', was about twenty years younger than Cadfael. 'They were old enemies, in so far as Brother Cadfael entertained enmities. He abhorred a sickly-pale tonsure.' 'A meagre man in the flesh was Brother Jerome, but he made up for it in zeal, though there were those who found that zeal too narrowly channelled, and somewhat dehydrated of the milk of human tolerance.'

Brother Richard, the sub-prior, was Robert's assistant and as such shared the responsibility for order and the observance of discipline in the monastery. Between them, as Radulfus says in the *Eighth Chronicle (The Devil's Novice)*, they bore 'the daily weight of the household and family'. The sub-prior, however, was the antithesis of Prior Robert, 'large, ungainly, amiable and benevolent, of good mind, but mentally lazy'; a 'good man at managing day-to-day affairs, but indolent at attempting decisions'.

Brother Matthew, the cellarer, was in charge of the abbey's stores, and as such was responsible for the purchase of everything concerning food, drink, fuel and other basic requirements. He also looked after the mills, brewhouse, bakery and many other buildings and estates belonging to the monastery. Chapter thirty-one of the Rule says that he is to 'have charge of all affairs, but he is not to act without the abbot's approval, and must carry out his orders'.

Brother Ambrose, the cellarer's clerk, always collected the yearly rents 'within the town and suburbs of Shrewsbury in person. No one knew the abbey rolls as Brother Ambrose did.' In 1140 he had been Matthew's clerk for about four years 'during which time fresh grants to the abbey had been flooding in richly, a new mill on the Tern, pastures, assarts, messuages in the town, glebes in the countryside, a fishery up-river, even a church or two, and there was no one who could match him at putting a finger on the slippery tenant or the field-lawyer, or the householder who had always three good stories to account for his inability to pay'.

Brother Anselm, the precentor, 'scholar and historian', made all the arrangements for the church services and was responsible not only for the music and the readings but also for training the monks to sing, ordering processions and looking after the service books. Anselm 'had his workshop in a corner carrel of the north walk of the cloister, where he kept the manuscripts of his music in neat and loving store'.

> [The] precentor, who also presided over the library, was ten years younger than Cadfael, a vague, unworldly man except where his personal enthusiasms were concerned, but alert and subtle enough in anything that concerned books, music or the instruments that make music, best of all the most perfect, the human voice. The blue eyes that peered out beneath his bushy brown eyebrows and shock of shaggy brown hair might be short-sighted, but they missed very little that went on, and had a tolerant twinkle for fallible human creatures and their failings, especially among the young.

The monk responsible for the welfare of all the abbey's guests was Brother Denis, the hospitaller, 'whose duties kept him most of the time around the court, and within sight of the gate'. Denis, with his 'round, rosy, tonsured head' and sharp brown eyes, 'had a retentive memory and an appetite for news and rumours that usually kept him the best-informed person in the enclave. The fuller his halls, the more pleasure he took in knowing everything that went on there, and the name and vocations of every guest. He also kept meticulous books to record the visitations.'

A 'child of the cloister from his fourth year' and only eight years younger than Cadfael, Brother Edmund, the infirmarer, was responsible for the care of the sick and 'old, retired brothers in the infirmary'. 'Meticulous in observation', Edmund was 'a grave, handsome, thoughtful creature who might have looked equally well on horseback and in arms, or farming a manor and keeping a patron's eye on his tenants'. Brother Cadfael, who regularly replenished the medicine-cupboard with his 'medicines, salves and febrifuges', was Edmund's 'closest friend and associate among the sick'. Standing at 'opposite poles of *oblatus* and *conversus*', herbalist and infirmarer 'understood each other so well that few words ever needed to pass between them'.

Brother Benedict, the sacristan, was essentially 'responsible for the upkeep of the church and enclave', including the contents of the church, its furniture, fittings and supplies. Sometimes, during the sacristan's 'long-winded legal haverings', Cadfael would quietly doze behind his pillar in the chapter-house.

*Gaye Orchard,*
*Shrewsbury Abbey*

*The lush level land known as the Gaye lay outside the loop of the River Severn, stretching from the English bridge to almost opposite Shrewsbury Castle. Today much of the land is occupied by the Gaye Meadow, the home ground of Shrewsbury Town Football Club. To the north and east lie the sprawling railway lines and sidings of Shrewsbury station. At the southern corner is a small park called the Abbey Gardens, sandwiched between the football ground, the Wakeman School and the abbey side of the English bridge.*

Brother Ambrose (not the cellarer's clerk of the same name) held the office of almoner, which 'brought him into contact with the poorest of the poor throughout the Foregate'. Every religious house was obliged to look after the needy and it was Ambrose's responsibility to distribute alms to those who queued up each day outside the abbey gates for food, clothing and sometimes money and medicine.

Brother Paul was not only the master of the novices and the boys, 'but the chief of their confessors, too'. He had 'never engendered, christened, nursed, tended young of his own, and yet there had been some quality in him that the old Abbot Heribert, no subtle nor very wise man, had rightly detected, and confided to him the boys and the novices in a trust he had never betrayed'. Although Paul was a good teacher, it

> had always been Brother Jerome's contention, frequently and vociferously expressed, that Brother Paul exercised far too slack an authority over his young charges, both the novices and the children. It was Paul's way to make his supervision of their days as unobtrusive as possible except when actually teaching, though he was prompt to appear if any of them needed or wanted him. But such routine matters as their ablutions, their orderly behaviour at meals, and their retiring at night and rising in the morning were left to their good consciences and to the sound habits of cleanliness and punctuality they had been taught. Brother Jerome was convinced that no boy under sixteen could be trusted to keep any rule, and that even those who had reached the mature age still had more of the devil in them than of the angels. He would have watched and hounded and corrected their every movement, had he been master of the boys, and made a great deal more use of punishments than ever Paul could be brought to contemplate.

Brother Eluric, custodian of Saint Mary's altar in the Lady Chapel, was, like Brother Edmund the infirmarer, 'a child of the cloister'. Aged about twenty in 1140, Eluric was 'the most learned and devout of his contemporaries, a tall, well-made young man, black-haired and black-eyed. He had been in the cloister since he was three years old, and knew nothing outside it. Unacquainted with sin, he was all the more haunted by it, as by some unknown monster, and assiduous in confession, he picked to pieces his own infinitesimal failings, with the mortal penitence due to deadly sins.'

Brother Petrus, a man who 'could not relax his hold on perfection', had been Abbot Heribert's cook long before he served Radulfus. Cadfael 'was one of a dozen or so people' within the abbey walls 'who were not afraid of Brother Petrus. Fanatics are always frightening, and Brother Petrus was a fanatic, not for his religion or his vocation, those he took for granted, but for his art. His dedicated fire tinted black hair and black eyes, scorching both with a fiery red. His northern blood boiled like his own cauldron. His temper, barbarian from the borders, was as hot as his own oven.'

Although seldom, if ever, mentioned in the *Chronicles*, there were a number of other obedientiaries who had specific responsibilities within the monastery: the succentor was the precentor's assistant; the sub-sacristan was responsible for ringing the bell for each of the services throughout the day and was the sacristan's chief helper; the chamberlain, an official not mentioned in Benedict's original Rule, was in charge of the care of clothes and linen (among his numerous other responsibilities was the duty to provide hot water and soap for washing and shaving); the kitchener was in charge of the cooking of food in the kitchens; and the fraterer looked after the refectory, its equipment, service and meals.

Brother Cadfael was an 'elderly and ordinary monk', and 'held no trouble-some parchment office'; 'within the Benedictine Rule, and in genial companion-ship with it, he had perfected a daily discipline of his own, that suited his needs admirably'. As Ellis Peters says in her introduction to *A Rare Benedictine*, although Cadfael may on occasions break the rules for what he feels to be good reasons, 'he will never transgress against the Rule, and never abandon it'.

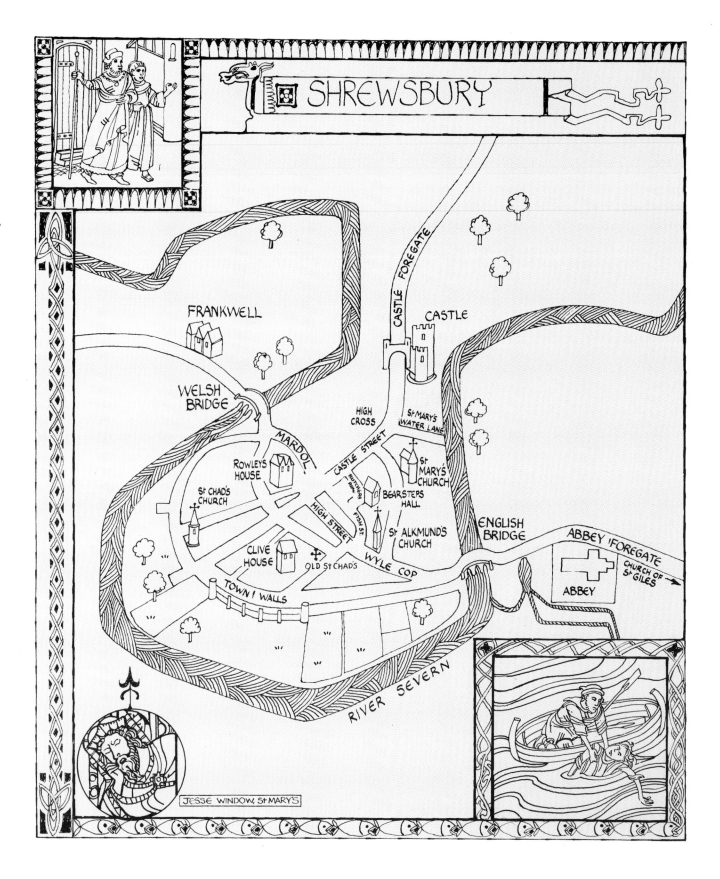

# SHREWSBURY

FRANKWELL

CASTLE FOREGATE

CASTLE

WELSH BRIDGE

HIGH CROSS

St MARY'S WATER LANE

MARDOL

ROWLEYS HOUSE

St CHAD'S CHURCH

CASTLE STREET

BUTCHERS ROW

St MARY'S CHURCH

BEARSTEPS HALL

HIGH STREET

FISH St.

St ALKMUND'S CHURCH

ENGLISH BRIDGE

ABBEY FOREGATE

CHURCH OF St GILES

CLIVE HOUSE

OLD St CHAD'S

WYLE COP

ABBEY

TOWN WALLS

RIVER SEVERN

JESSE WINDOW, St MARY'S

# Shrewsbury

The longest river in Britain, the Severn, rises on Plynlimon in the mountains of central Wales to flow, in a huge semicircular curve, to the Bristol Channel and the Atlantic Ocean. Beginning as a mountain stream and ending as a tidal estuary, its approximate 200-mile journey takes it north-eastward, through Powys to Welshpool and across the Welsh border into Shropshire. The first English town on the river is Shrewsbury, situated in 'a close loop of the Severn', and the place where most of the *Chronicles of Brother Cadfael* are set. From Shrewsbury the river winds south across the Shropshire plain, past the Wrekin, through the Ironbridge Gorge to Bridgnorth and on through the counties of Hereford and Worcester and Gloucester to the sea.

During the nineteenth century barges, travelling from as far away as Bristol, could reach Welshpool. But today the recommended upper limit for navigation is Stourport-on-Severn, about seventeen miles down river from Bridgnorth. In the *Fourth Chronicle (Saint Peter's Fair)*, set in the summer of 1139, boats came to Shrewsbury from Gloucester, Buildwas, Brigge (Bridgnorth) and even Wales. One 'fellow, by the name of Rhodri ap Huw, from Mold', in Clwyd, brought his wool-clip, including honey, mead and hides, to Saint Peter's fair by boat; 'a great load', which he shipped up the River Dee and then had transported, at considerable expense, overland to the River Vrnwy (Vyrnwy), a tributary of the Severn. Thomas of Bristol, too, brought his wares by river to the annual Shrewsbury fair. He was 'a man of consequence in the city of Bristol', in 'very good odour with Robert of Gloucester' (the half-brother of the Empress Maud), and was 'one of the biggest importers of wine into the port there'.

Although Shrewsbury lies only five miles north-west of the Roman city of

*River Severn at Shrewsbury*

Viroconium (Wroxeter), no evidence of Roman occupation has been found in the town. Its origins, however, date back at least to Saxon times. In his writings, Llywarc Hen, a sixth-century poet, refers to Shrewsbury by its Welsh name of Pengwern, meaning 'the hill of alders'. It is reputed that Brocwael, King of Powys, had a palace on the hill where the old Church of Saint Chad now stands. By the ninth century, however, the settlement was part of the kingdom of Mercia, and known by the Anglo-Saxon name of Scrobbesbyrig, probably meaning the 'town on the shrub-covered hill'. Some historians, however, have suggested that Scrobbes is a personal name.

Towards the end of the ninth century, King Alfred the Great granted Mercia to his son-in-law, Ethelred, and on this nobleman's death in about 910 his widow, Ethelfleda, Alfred's eldest daughter, ruled as the 'Lady of the Mercians'. By this time Shrewsbury was an important administrative centre in the Severn valley, and was guarded by a timber fortification at the narrow neck of land where the castle now stands. Ethelfleda, who died in 918, spent the rest of her reign trying to defend her kingdom from Welsh border hostilities and Danish incursions, building numerous fortifications, including castles at Quatford (near Bridgnorth) and Chirbury (near Montgomery). According to tradition, she frequently visited Shrewsbury, where she founded the church dedicated to Saint Alkmund, a prince of the royal house of Northumbria, from which she herself was descended.

In 924 Aethelstan, the eldest son of Edward the Elder, succeeded his father as King of Wessex and Mercia, and in the following year he passed a law to unify the coinage throughout his empire, by specifying the number of moneyers allowed in certain towns or cities. Henceforth, in addition to the previous practice of including the name of the moneyer on the coin, the place where it was struck was also to be included. Shrewsbury was one of the places allowed to mint coins and examples of these still exist. In 1936 a hoard of coins of Edward the Elder, from the early tenth century, was discovered during excavations near the castle.

In the *Seventh Chronicle (The Sanctuary Sparrow)* Brother Cadfael discovers in Shrewsbury a silver penny struck in the reign of the Confessor, 'the sainted Edward, King before the Normans came, a beautiful piece minted in this town. The moneyer was one Godesbrond, there are a few of his pieces to be found, but few indeed in the town where they were struck.'

The Domesday Survey of 1086 shows that, in the reign of Edward the Confessor, Shrewsbury had 252 houses, each inhabited by a burgess, and a population of nearly a thousand (including Godesbrond and two other moneyers). In pre-Norman times the town was probably surrounded by defensive earthworks, while most of the dwellings were of timber construction. There were five principal churches: four built of stone – Saint Chad's, Saint Alkmund's,

*Old Saint Chad's, Shrewsbury*

*The first Church of Saint Chad is reputed to have been founded at the end of the eighth century by Offa, King of Mercia. It was recorded in the Norman survey of 1086 as holding, in addition to other lands and tithes in Shropshire, one and a half hides of land (about 180 acres) in Shrewsbury. The collegiate church was not dissolved until the reign of Edward VI. It continued to be used as a parish church until 9 July 1788 when the tower and the north side of the building collapsed. Although large sections of the church remained standing, the building was demolished in 1789, except for the Lady Chapel, now known as Old Saint Chad's.*

Saint Mary's and Saint Julian's – and one built of wood (St Peter's), which stood outside the loop of the river on the site where the abbey now stands (see Shrewsbury Abbey, p. 69).

After the Norman invasion of 1066, William the Conqueror allowed Earl Edwin of Mercia, grandson of Leofric and Lady Godiva, to retain his Midland kingdom, which included Shrewsbury. A few years later, however, the Earl joined an unsuccessful Anglo-Welsh rebellion against the Normans, led by Edric Syvaticus, or Edric the Wild. According to Ordericus Vitalis, himself a native of Shrewsbury, Earl Edwin, attempting to avenge his brother's imprisonment by the Normans, was 'slain on the banks of a river, from which he could not escape, on account of a high tide'.

Shortly after the death of Edwin, William the Conqueror conferred the earldom of Shrewsbury upon his kinsman Roger de Montgomery, the founder of the Abbey of Saint Peter and Saint Paul. In about 1070 Earl Roger began to enlarge and strengthen the wooden fortifications at Shrewsbury, and in the process of clearing the ground to provide more space, over a hundred houses were demolished. It is from this stronghold that Earl Roger led campaigns into the Welsh borderlands. From here, too, in 1088, rebelling against William Rufus, Earl Roger led an 'ill-assorted army' (according to Owen and Blakeway's *A History of Shrewsbury*) in an unsuccessful attempt to capture Worcester.

Earl Roger died in 1094, having made peace with Rufus, and his possessions were divided between his two sons: Hugh de Montgomery inherited his Shropshire lands and became the Second Earl of Shrewsbury, while Robert de Bellême inherited his estates in Normandy. Earl Hugh also inherited a land torn by warfare, for, in 1094, according to Owen and Blakeway, 'Shropshire was laid waste by the Welsh incursions under the command of Griffith ap Cynan, King of North Wales, and Cadwgaun, Prince of Powis; and in the following year they destroyed the castle of Montgomery'. When Earl Hugh was killed in a battle against Danish invaders in 1098, Robert de Belleme, having paid William Rufus a large sum of money for the privilege, became the Third Earl of Shrewsbury.

Earl Robert strengthened not only his castle at Shrewsbury but also those at Montgomery and Ludlow, and in addition built a new castle at Bridgnorth. When Robert of Normandy, brother of King Henry I, invaded England in 1101, Robert de Bellême rallied to his side. Bloodshed, however, was avoided by a peaceful settlement and, in the following year, Henry marched north into Mercia to rid himself of the rebellious Earl and his followers. He captured the castle at Bridgnorth and forced Earl Robert to surrender at Shrewsbury. Robert de Bellême, who confessed to treason, was banished from the country and his castles, lands and properties were forfeited to the Crown (see King Stephen and the Empress Maud, p. 25).

*The great hall,
Shrewsbury Castle*

*Window on south side of the
great hall, Shrewsbury Castle*

*Apart from the Norman gateway, very little survives of the original Norman castle of Shrewsbury, founded by Earl Roger de Montgomery in about 1070, as Edward I, rebuilding and strengthening the castle in about 1300, demolished much of the Norman building and added an outer bailey. It was never used as a fortress after this date and, over the centuries, was allowed to fall into disrepair. Queen Elizabeth I gave the castle to the bailiffs and burgesses of Shrewsbury in 1586 and little was done to the building until the Civil War, when further alterations were made. The interior of the great hall was partitioned and extra floors were constructed, including an upper floor lit by a row of square mullioned windows on the south side. The doors in the main gateway date from this time. It was captured by the Parliamentarians in 1645 and it was not until 1660, when Charles II was restored to the throne, that it was surrendered to the Crown. The King granted the castle to Sir Francis Newport of High Ercall, Shropshire, in 1663 and it remained in private hands until 1924, when it was acquired by the Corporation of Shrewsbury. It was restored as much as possible to its Edwardian condition and opened to the public in 1926.*

*Laura's Tower,*
*Shrewsbury Castle*

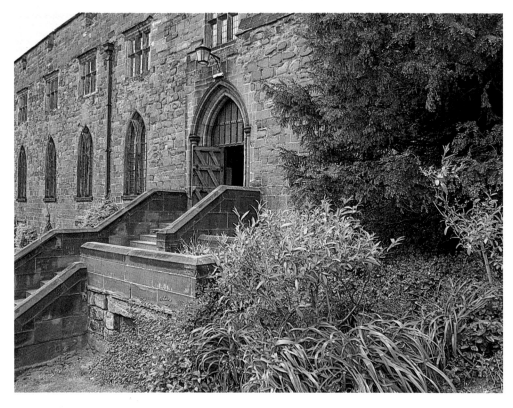

*Doorway to the great hall,*
*Shrewsbury Castle*

By 1100, the year when Henry seized the crown of England to become King, Shrewsbury already had two bridges over the Severn: the Welsh Bridge and the English Bridge, which was probably built by the monks of the nearby Benedictine abbey. The first record of the town being enclosed by stone walls was in the thirteenth century, during the reign of Henry III. It is thought, however, that the town had walled defences long before this. Owen and Blakeway state that it 'must have been at least surrounded with a rampart of earth, when Aethelstan gave it the privilege of a minter, and when Edgar or Ethelred honoured it with their residence; and that rampart, in all probability, pursued nearly the same circuit which was afterwards adopted by the masons of Henry III'.

In the *Fourth Chronicle (Saint Peter's Fair)*, set a year after the damage caused to the town by Stephen's storming of the castle in 1138, a delegation from the Guild Merchants of Shrewsbury appealed to the abbey 'to set aside a proportion of the fair tolls on goods, whether by horse-load or cart or boat, to be handed over to the town, and spent on restoring the walls'.

Under Henry I Shrewsbury was granted its first charter, but the terms have been lost. The King visited the town in about 1115 and in 1126 he gave it to his second wife, Adeliza, who appointed William FitzAlan as Sheriff to look after her interests in the shire. During the 'civil war for the crown of England' which followed Henry's death in 1135, FitzAlan held Shrewsbury Castle for the Empress Maud. The *Second Chronicle (One Corpse Too Many)* is based on King Stephen's siege and conquest of this Midland stronghold. FitzAlan managed to escape to Normandy, but in 1154, when Stephen died and the Empress's son became King Henry II, he returned to England and was 're-instated in all his vast possessions, both in Shropshire and elsewhere' (Owen and Blakeway).

The *Chronicles* begin in 1137 (one year before the siege and capture of Shrewsbury by King Stephen) and proceed 'steadily season by season, year by year', describing life not only in the Benedictine monastery but also in the medieval town.

At Shrewsbury the river 'made a great moat about the walls, turning the town almost into an island, but for the neck of land covered and protected by the castle'. There were 'only two bridges, one towards the abbey and London' and 'one towards Wales, with a fan of roads branching out westwards'. The eastern bridge, known as the English Bridge because it was on the English side of the town, was stone-built with a drawbridge that 'could cut off approach to the town at need'. Under the first arch of the bridge there used to be moored a boat-mill, the mooring chain of which, during the period of the *Chronicles*, was still in evidence, bolted to a ring in the stone. From this chain FitzAlan's treasury was hidden beneath the waters of the Severn, until it was removed and returned to its rightful owner in the *Second Chronicle (One Corpse Too Many)*.

*Meole Brook in the frost*

*Norman gateway,*
*Shrewsbury Castle*

'*Where the causeway swept up from the street to the gate of the castle, the beggars who followed the king's camp had taken up new stations, hopeful and expectant, for the king's justiciar, Bishop Robert of Salisbury, had arrived to join his master, and brought a train of wealthy and important clerics with him. In the lee of the gate-house wall Lame Osbern's little trolley was drawn up, where he could beg comfortably without having to move. The worn wooden pattens he used for his callused knuckles lay tidily beside him on the trolley, on top of the folded black cloak he would not need until night fell. It was so folded that the bronze clasp at the neck showed up proudly against the black, the dragon of eternity with his tail in his mouth.*'

*One Corpse Too Many*

*'Meantime, Cadfael went up to Saint Mary's churchyard, and sought out the venerable beggar who sat beside the west door, in his privileged and honoured place. Rhodri the Less – for his father had been Rhodri, too, and a respected beggar like his son – knew the footstep, and turned up a wrinkled and pock-marked face, brown as the soil, smiling.*

*"Brother Cadfael, well met, and what's the news with you?"*

*'Cadfael sat down beside him, and chatted with the blind old man for a while about Master William Rede, Brother Matthew's chief steward, who was attacked the previous night while collecting the abbey rents in the passage between Saint Mary's and the water-gate.*

*'Rhodri leaned to rattle his begging-bowl at the pious lady who had been putting up prayers in the church. Business was business, and the pitch he held was the envy of the beggars of Shrewsbury. He blessed the giver, and reached a delaying hand to halt Cadfael, who was rising to depart.'*

*A Rare Benedictine: Eye Witness*

*The south side of Saint Mary's Church, Shrewsbury*

Brother Cadfael's 'friend and fellow Welshman, Madog of the Dead Boat, who knew everything there was to be known about water and its properties', was a familiar sight on the Severn. He 'had got his name as a result of the cargo he most often had to carry, by reason of his knowledge of all the places where missing persons, thought to have been taken by the river whether in flood or felony, were likely to fetch up'. Madog received 'a fee for every Christian body' he brought out of the water; 'he had indeed a right to it. The duty had edged its way in on him long ago, almost unaware, but other men's dying was the better part of his living now. And an honest, useful, decent art, for which many a family had been thankful.'

Madog of the Dead Boat, who could 'outswim most fish', had a 'hut tucked under the lee of the western bridge that opened the road into his native Wales, and there he made coracles, or timber boats if required, fished in season, ferried fares on request, carried goods for a fee, anything to do with transport by water'.

The suburb of Frankwell lay at the end of the western bridge, outside the town walls and over the river. Beyond Frankwell, Walter Aurifaber, a wealthy Shrewsbury goldsmith, owned 'a pasture and a stable', and it is there that his daughter, Susanna, was killed by an arrow loosed by one of the Sheriff's marksmen in the *Seventh Chronicle*. According to the *Sixteenth Chronicle (The Heretic's Apprentice)*:

> The workshop where Jevan of Lythwood treated his sheepskins lay well beyond the last houses of the suburb of Frankwell, solitary by the right bank of the river, at the foot of a steep meadow backed by a ridge of trees and bushes higher up the slope. Here the land rose, and the water, even at its summer level, ran deep, and with a rapid and forceful current, ideal for Jevan's occupation. The making of vellum demanded an unfailing supply of water, for the first several days of the process running water, and this spot where the Severn ran rapidly provided perfect anchorage for the open wooden frames covered with netting, in which the raw skins were fastened, so that the water could flow freely down the whole length of them, day and night, until they were ready to go into a solution of lime and water in which they would spend a fortnight, before being scraped clean of all remaining hair, and another fortnight afterwards to complete the long bleaching.

From the abbey – sited outside the town walls on the eastern bank of the Severn – Brother Cadfael made regular journeys into the town to attend his patients or visit his friend Hugh Beringar, who was initially Deputy Sheriff of Shropshire and later Sheriff. In 1141 he found himself making one such journey:

> There was no real need for Cadfael to deliver the herbs and medicines in person, but he took advantage of the opportunity as much to satisfy his curiosity as to enjoy the walk and the fresh air on a fine, if blustery, March day. Along the Foregate, over the bridge spanning the Severn, muddied and turgid from the thaw in the mountains, in

through the town gate, up the long, steep curve of the Wyle, and gently downhill from the High Cross to the castle gatehouse, he went with eyes and ears alert, stopping many times to exchange greetings and pass the time of day.

The town gate 'on the eastern side was a part of the castle defences', and was 'closed and guarded during the night hours'. Since King Stephen's siege,

> Shrewsbury had been safe enough from any threat on the eastern approach, only the occasional brief Welsh raid from the west had troubled the peace of the shire, but Hugh Beringar maintained the routine watchfulness without a break. But the most easterly wicket, giving access to the river under the very towers of the fortress, was there to be used freely. Only in times of possible danger were all the wickets closed and barred, and sentries set on the walls. Horsemen, carts, market wagons, all must wait for the gates to be opened at dawn, but a solitary man might pass through at any hour.

Outside the northern gate of Shrewsbury 'the Castle Foregate housed a tight little suburb of houses and shops, but it ended very soon, and gave place to meadows on either side the road.' Here the 'river twined serpentine coils on both sides, beyond the fields', and 'in the first level meadow on the left' Hugh Beringar fought a duel to the death with Adam Courcelle, Deputy Sheriff of Shropshire in the *Second Chronicle*.

*High Cross, Shrewsbury*

Lame Osbern, one of the town beggars, had his pitch outside the castle gates. He 'had been born with both legs withered, and scuttled around at unbelievable speed on hands provided with wooded pattens, dragging his shrivelled knees behind him on a little wheeled trolley'. In the *Second Chronicle* Cadfael presented him with a thick, warm cloak.

Up until his death in March 1141, Gilbert Prestcote, Sheriff of Shropshire, had made his family apartments high in the corner tower of the castle. His successor, Hugh Beringar, however, had preferred to maintain a residence in the town. He lived with his wife, Aline, and their son, Giles, in a house by Saint Mary's Church, 'only up the curve of the Wyle and the level street beyond'.

Several old streets in Shrewsbury were named after the traders who lived or carried out their business in them: Butcher Row, Milk Street, Fish Street, all survive today. Other names, however, have disappeared: Corviser's or Shoe-maker's Row is now known as Pride Hill, while Baker's or Baxter's Row has been swallowed by the High Street. Nevertheless, all of the street names mentioned in the *Chronicles* still exist (their layout, too, has hardly changed): the Wyle (its summit known as the Wyle Cop) is a long, steep, winding road that climbs uphill from the eastern gate towards the High Cross (it was in this street that Martin Bellecote, master carpenter, lived with his wife and family); High Street runs between the Wyle and Maerdol-head; Butcher Row lies midway between the High Street and Saint Mary's Church and is where Edric Flesher,

*St Mary's Church from the altar to the west door, Shrewsbury*

*The Norman south door of St Mary's Church, Shrewsbury*

In about 970, after King Edgar had made it a royal chapel, with a dean, seven prebends and a parish priest, St Mary's Church was rebuilt on the site of probably two earlier Saxon churches. It remained a collegiate church, with the King as its patron, until the Dissolution when in 1547–48 it became a parish church. It continued, however, to be a royal chapel until 1846. The Saxon church was demolished during the reign of Henry II (1153–1189), and in its place a cruciform Norman church without aisles was constructed of red sandstone. The Trinity Chapel was added in about 1360, and the central tower removed in about 1471 and a clerestory built from the east end of the church to the west. The octagonal stone spire, reaching a height of over 138 feet, partly collapsed in 1894 and was rebuilt. The church was extensively restored in Victorian times. St Mary's is the largest church in Shrewsbury, measuring 185 feet in length.

'chief of the butchers of Shrewsbury', had his shop; the burgage of Walter Aurifaber, the goldsmith, was 'situated on the street leading to the gateway of the castle' (Castle Street); while the Vestiers, 'the biggest and best-known clothiers in Shrewsbury', had a house and shop at Mardol-head (Maerdol). According to the *Thirteenth Chronicle (The Rose Rent)*:

> The burgage of the Vestier family occupied a prominent place at the head of the street called Maerdol, which led downhill to the western bridge. A right-angled house, with wide shop-front on the street, and the long stem of the hall and chambers running well back behind, with a spacious yard and stables. There was room enough in all that elongated building, besides the living rooms of the family, to house ample stores in a good dry undercroft, and provide space for all the girls who carded and combed the newly dyed wool, besides three horizontal looms set up in their own outbuilding, and plenty of room in the long hall for half a dozen spinsters at once. Others worked in their own homes, and so did five other weavers about the town.

A wool merchant's town property is described in the *Sixteenth Chronicle*:

> The house of Girard of Lythwood, like so many of the merchant burgages of Shrewsbury, was in the shape of an L, the short base directly on the street, and pierced by an arched entry leading through to the yard and garden behind. The base of the L was of only one storey, and provided the shop where Jevan, the younger brother, stored and sold his finished leaves and gatherings of vellum and the cured skins from which they were folded and cut to order. The upright of the L showed its gable end to the street, and consisted of a low undercroft and the living floor above, with a loft in the steep roof that provided extra sleeping quarters. The entire burgage was not large, space being valuable within so enclosed a town, in its tight noose of river. Outside the loop, in the suburbs of Frankwell on one side and the Foregate on the other, there was room to expand, but within the wall every inch of ground had to be used to the best advantage.

Ralph Giffard, 'the Lord of two or three country manors', owned a town house near Saint Chad's Church, where he preferred to spend his winters in comfort. According to the *Twelfth Chronicle (The Raven in the Foregate)*:

> He had lost one manor through loyalty to the cause of his overlord FitzAlan and his sovereign, the Empress Maud, and it had taken him a good deal of cautious treading and quiet submission to achieve the successful retention of what remained. He had but one cause that mattered to him now, and that was to preserve his own situation and leave his remaining estate intact to his son. His life had never been threatened, he had not been so deeply involved as to invite death. But possessions are possessions, and he was an ageing man, by no means minded to abandon his lands and flee either abroad, to Normandy or Anjou, where he had no status, or to Gloucester, to take up arms for the liege lady who had already cost him dear. No, better far to sit still, shun every tempter, and forget old allegiance. Only so he could ensure that young Ralph [his son], . . . playing the lord of the manor at home, should survive this long conflict for the crown without loss, no matter which of the two claimants finally triumphed.

By the middle of the twelfth century, the period of the *Chronicles*, Shrewsbury was a charter borough, where, in Cadfael's words, 'the unfree may work their way to freedom in a year and a day. And sensible boroughs encourage the coming of good craftsmen, and will go far to hide and protect them.' Among those to take advantage of the chance to earn their freedom were the villein Harald, who was taken on by 'a farrier on the town side of the western bridge'; and Alard the silversmith, who had escaped from his brutal master, Hamo FitzHamon of Lidyate, and been hidden by the merchants of the town until he was a free man.

Between the main streets in Shrewsbury, in medieval times, there existed a warren of shuts and passages, and despite the enormous changes that have taken place in the town throughout the intervening centuries, a considerable number have survived. The word 'shut', according to J.B. Blakeway (Salop MSS 1817), is 'not, as might be imagined, a cul-de-sac or alley shut at one end, but, on the contrary, one open at both extremes, enabling the pedestrian, for it is previous only to such, to shoot or move rapidly from one street into another'. Others, however, have suggested that the word may be derived from 'Schutte', the name of a family who once owned a house in Drayton's Passage. Although the origins of some of the names of these shuts and passages are obscure, among those that have survived there are a few worthy of note: Bear Steps, Plough Shut, Compasses Passage, Golden Cross Passage, Barracks Passage, Saint Mary's Shut, and, two with particularly graphic names, Gullet Passage and Grope Lane.

The *Chronicles* suggest that there were a number of alehouses in the town, and mention two in particular: one in Mardol and another in 'a narrow, secluded close off the upper end of the steep, descending Wyle'. It was sited about midway between 'Saint Alkmund's church and the town gate, and the lanes leading to it were shut between high walls'. Outside the town walls, in the extensive parish of Holy Cross to the east of Shrewsbury, there was an inn owned by Walter Renold, better known as Wat's tavern. It 'lay at the far corner of the horse-fair, not on the London highroad, but on the quieter road that bore away north-eastwards' and 'was handy for the country people who brought goods to market'.

A number of alehouses were situated in the Abbey Foregate itself, and alongside them were the houses and shops of the local tradesmen. Among these were the premises of Erwald the wheelwright, who was provost of the Foregate; the bakery of Jordan Achard, who 'bakes good bread, and never cheats on the weight'; the forge of Thomas the farrier; and the workshop and house of Niall the bronzesmith, rented to the abbey by Judith Perle, née Vestier, for an annual payment of one white rose.

*St Alkmund's Church from the west door to the altar, Shrewsbury*

*St Alkmund's Church, Shrewsbury*

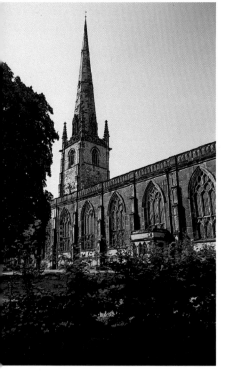

The Church of St Alkmund dates from Saxon times and is thought to have been founded by Ethelfleda, the 'Lady of the Mercians'. It became a collegiate church during the reign of King Edgar (957–975). At the time of the Norman Conquest, its parish was one of four in Shrewsbury: the others being St Chad's, St Julian's and St Mary's. The church was granted to Richard de Belmeis and, when he and his brother Philip founded Lilleshall Abbey in about 1148, much of the wealth of St Alkmund's went towards the building and maintenance of the abbey. After the collapse of Old St Chad's in 1788, it was decided to pull down and rebuild the medieval church of St Alkmund, except for the 184 foot high spire dating from the fifteenth century. The new building was designed by Carline and Tilley and was completed in 1795.

There were few inhabitants of the parish of Holy Cross that Brother Cadfael did not know:

> He had treated many of them, or their children, at some time in these his cloistered years; even, sometimes, their beasts, for he who learns about sickness of men cannot but pick up, here and there, some knowledge of the sicknesses of their animals, creatures with as great a capacity for suffering as their masters, and much less means of complaining, together with far less inclination to complain. Cadfael often wished that men would use their beasts better, and tried to show them that it would be good husbandry. The horses of war had been part of that curious, slow process within him that had turned him at length from trade in arms into the cloister (see Brother Cadfael, p. 19).

In addition to knowing many of the parishioners of Holy Cross, there was also very little about the abbey precinct and the town of Shrewsbury that Cadfael did not know. As Hugh Beringar good-humouredly remarked to him one day before Mass: 'How many eyes and ears have you in every street in Shrewsbury? I wish my own intelligencers knew half as much of what goes on'.

To Cadfael, people were endlessly mysterious and, as he himself admitted, 'I am endlessly curious. A sin to be confessed, no doubt, and well worth a penance. As long as man is curious about his fellowman, that appetite alone will keep him alive.' And, as the *Chronicles* reveal, there was always plenty going on in the town of Shrewsbury to 'satisfy his curiosity', particularly when it came to solving crimes.

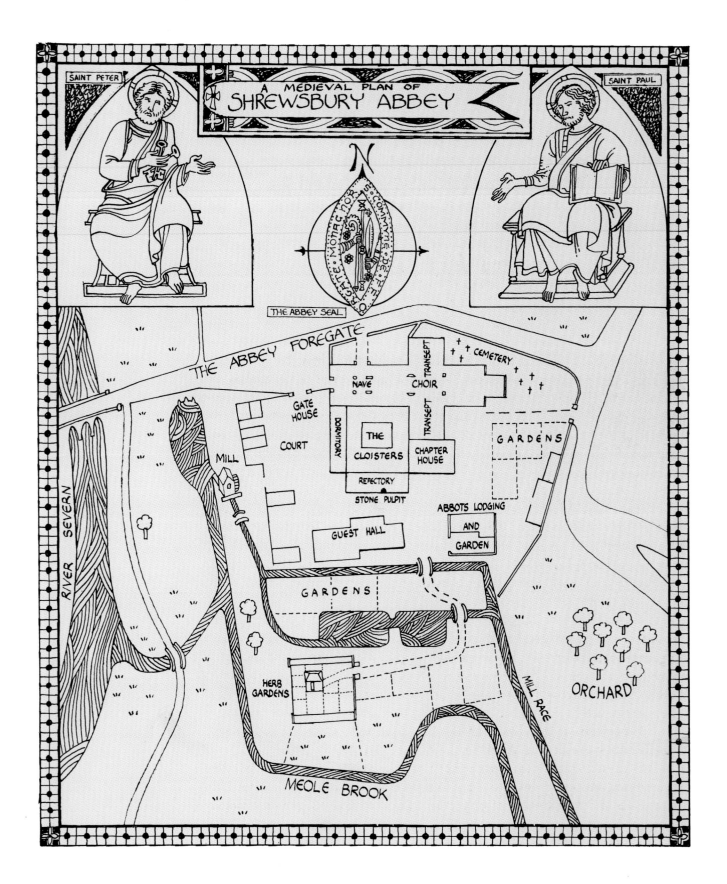

A MEDIEVAL PLAN OF SHREWSBURY ABBEY

SAINT PETER

SAINT PAUL

THE ABBEY SEAL

THE ABBEY FOREGATE

RIVER SEVERN

GATE HOUSE

COURT

MILL

DORMITORY

THE CLOISTERS

REFECTORY

STONE PULPIT

NAVE

CHOIR

TRANSEPT

TRANSEPT

CHAPTER HOUSE

CEMETERY

GARDENS

ABBOTS LODGING AND GARDEN

GUEST HALL

GARDENS

HERB GARDENS

MILL RACE

ORCHARD

MEOLE BROOK

# Shrewsbury Abbey

 hortly after the Norman Conquest William the Conqueror rewarded Roger de Montgomery, the son of his cousin, not only with lands and an earldom in the south of England but also with the earldom of Shrewsbury, which included the town and nearly all of Shropshire. Earl Roger, who also held a number of estates and titles in Normandy, subsequently became one of the most powerful noblemen in England and was responsible for building Shrewsbury Castle and parts of Wenlock Priory. In 1082 his chaplain and adviser, Odelirius, who had accompanied him to England and become priest of the small wooden church of Saint Peter, east of Shrewsbury town, made a pilgrimage to Rome. Impressed by the splendour and scale of the church architecture there, he vowed that if he should return safely to Shrewsbury he would replace his small wooden church with one built of stone, in honour of the two apostles Saint Peter and Saint Paul.

Earl Roger received Odelirius's idea of building a new and grander church across the river with great enthusiasm and, recognising the benefits that a monastery would bring to the people and town of Shrewsbury, he immediately determined to found a religious house of the Benedictine Order. In March 1083, in the presence of many witnesses, the Earl vowed that he would found an abbey on the site of the old wooden church, 'and granted thereunto the whole suburb lying without the eastern gate: which donation he confirmed by laying his gloves upon the altar' (H.E. Forrest, *The Old Churches of Shrewsbury*).

Monks were brought over from Seez in Normandy to supervise the building of the abbey, among them two Benedictines named Rainald and Frodo, 'no doubt selected for their skill in architecture' (Forrest). Work began immediately

*The south side of
Shrewsbury Abbey*

*Adjoining the south side of the
abbey church, before the
Dissolution, was the complex of
buildings that included the
cloisters, the chapter house, the
dormitory and the refectory.
During the late
nineteenth-century rebuilding
of the east end by John
Loughborough Pearson, the
remains of the south transept
were walled in and given three
lancet windows*

and continued for many years. In 1142, according to the *Chronicles of Brother Cadfael*, there 'were several among the brothers who had worked on the building of additions to the enclave, barns and stabling and storehouses'. Brother Conradin, in particular, who was 'still in his fifties and robust as a bull, had been one of the first child oblates, and worked as a boy under the monks of Seez'.

The *Chronicles* describe in colourful and fascinating detail the daily life and monastic routine of the Benedictine abbey at Shrewsbury during the middle years of the twelfth century. The buildings, lands and possessions of the monastery form the backdrop to many of the stories; indeed, most of the plots are derived from the abbey's 'true history'.

The original endowment to the monastery by Earl Roger was, according to Forrest, 'only moderate'. In addition to all the adjoining land, known as Monks' Foregate and later Abbey Foregate, the Domesday survey of 1086 recorded that the abbey held the manors of Eyton (near Wroxeter), Boreton (near Condover) and Emstrey, just over two miles south-east of Shrewsbury. It received income, however, from eight churches: Baschurch, Berrington, Corfham, Hodnet, Morville, Little Ness, Stottesdon and Wrockwardine. Before his death, in 1094, Earl Roger had added six more churches to the list: Condover, Donington, Edgmond, High Ercall, Tong and Wellington. He also granted the abbot the right to hold an annual fair at Lammas, the first day of August, for 'horned cattle, horses, cheese and linen' (Forrest). At the beginning of the year 1139 King Stephen confirmed this ancient charter, 'with all its grants in lands, rights and privileges'.

The *Fourth Chronicle (Saint Peter's Fair)* begins on the eve of this grand, festive event, held in 'the great triangle of the horse-fair, and all along the Foregate from the bridge to the corner of the enclosure, where the road veered right towards Saint Giles, and the king's highway to London'. Set in the summer of 1139, the *Chronicle* goes on to describe the scene:

> There was a newly-erected wooden jetty downstream from the bridge, where the long riverside stretch of the main abbey gardens and orchards began, the rich lowland known as the Gaye. By river, by road, afoot through the forests and over the border from Wales, traders of all kinds began to make their way to Shrewsbury. And into the great court of the abbey flocked all the gentry of the shire, and of neighbouring shires too, lordlings, knights, yeomen, with their wives and daughters . . . for the three days of the annual fair. Subsistence goods they grew, or bred, or brewed, or wove, or span for themselves, the year round, but once a year they came to buy the luxury cloths, the fine wines, the rare preserved fruits, the gold and silver work, all the treasures that appeared on the feast of Saint Peter ad Vincula, and vanished three days later. To these great fairs came merchants even from Flanders and Germany, shippers with French wines, shearers with the wool-clip from Wales, and clothiers with the finished goods, gowns, jerkins, hose, town fashions come to the country.

*Wenlock Priory*

'The roses had begun to bloom early, by reason of fine, warm weather. Spring rains had brought a good hay crop, and June ideal conditions for gathering it. The shearing was almost finished, and the wool dealers were reckoning up hopefully the value of their clips.'

*The Heretic's Apprentice*

After the foundation of the abbey, Earl Roger decreed that if he died in England he should be buried in the abbey church. Although some early historians claim that he was killed while fighting in Wales, it is more generally accepted that he died in the abbey. It seems that he was taken ill in Shrewsbury Castle and, sensing that his end was near, he was received as a monk, a lay-brother, on 14 July 1094. He died three days later and was 'honourably interred in the new church between the two altars, a situation which, at that period, not even his rank and munificence could have obtained for him, if he had not been invested with the monastic garb' (Forrest). His grave would have been at the extreme east end of the Norman church, between the High Altar and the original altar of the Lady Chapel. At the Dissolution this part of the church was demolished and, reputedly, all that is left of Earl Roger's tomb is a stone slab bearing his damaged effigy. This monument, the oldest in the church, is situated at the east end of the south aisle, near the entrance to the present Lady Chapel. Experts, however, have claimed that the effigy's armour is of a period at least a hundred years later than the time in which Earl Roger lived.

The first abbot, Fulchered, was appointed in 1087 and was described by Ordric, or Ordericus Vitalis, the eldest son of Odelirius, as an elegant preacher. According to Owen, Fulchered came from Seez in Normandy with three other Benedictines, 'and arrived naked and hungry at Shrewsbury'. He died in 1120 and was succeeded by Abbot Godefrid, who is mentioned briefly in *A Light on the Road to Woodstock (A Rare Benedictine)*. He died suddenly in 1127 and Prior Heribert, 'a modest man of comfortable figure and amiable countenance', whom Cadfael had freed from being kidnapped in November 1120, was made Abbot. It was Abbot Heribert who, in 1137, gave Prior Robert permission to mount an expedition into Wales to bring the bones of Saint Winifred back to Shrewsbury Abbey (see Saint Winifred, p. 85).

After the siege and fall of Shrewsbury Castle, according to the *Chronicles*, Abbot Heribert became, in King Stephen's eyes, 'the scapegoat for Shrewsbury's offence in holding out against his claims'. In December 1138 the Abbot startled everyone in the house by announcing that he was summoned to attend a 'legatine council in London for the reform of the church' to account for his '"stewardship as abbot. The terms make clear," said Heribert, firmly and sadly, "that my tenure is at the disposal of the legate. We have lived through a troubled year, and been tossed between two claimants to the throne of our land. It is not a secret, and I acknowledge it, that his Grace, when he was here in the summer, held me in no great favour, since in the confusion of the times I did not see my way clear, and was slow to accept his sovereignty. Therefore I now regard my abbacy as suspended, until or unless the legatine council confirms me in office."' The council, for whatever reason, judged that the Abbot should be replaced by Radulfus, who was an 'aristocrat and the equal of a baron', and Heribert was demoted to a 'simple brother' under the new Abbot. He died in the year 1140, having 'ended his days quite happily as a simple choir-monk, without regrets'.

Abbot Radulfus, showed himself 'both an austere but just disciplinarian and a shrewd and strong-minded businessman. He owed his preferment to the abbacy as much to the King as to the papal legate, and valued and feared for the order of the realm at least as keenly as for the state of his own cure.' During his tenure of office he made the decision to 'accept no more infants into the cloistered life decreed for them by others'. Prior Robert Pennant, who had always yearned for the mitre himself, had been 'sorely disappointed' when the legatine council had 'passed him over in favour of a stranger, to fill the vacancy left by the deposition of Abbot Heribert, but he had not given up hope'. In the end his patience was rewarded. When Radulfus died in 1148, he was appointed as his successor, and was Abbot of the Benedictine Abbey of Saint Peter and Saint Paul at Shrewsbury for nearly twenty years.

*Meole Brook*

*'Two threads of silver made the only sparkles of light in the muted sunbeams, the nearer one the mill leat drawn off to feed the abbey pools and mill, the further one the Meole brook itself, here in a stony and broken bed, and looking curiously small by comparison with its broad flow by the abbey gardens, barely a mile downstream.'*

The Leper of Saint Giles

Occupying a spur of high, dry land on the far east bank of the Severn, beyond the eastern gate of the town, the abbey grounds were surrounded on every side but one 'by a high boundary wall. The remaining side was bordered by the Meole Brook, no mean water hemming the gardens, but fordable or swimmable.' The Meole Brook, marked on modern Ordnance Survey maps as the Rea

*River Severn, near Atcham*

Brook, rises on the hills flanking the Minsterley valley. From its source near Marton, it winds north-east down the valley, passing Minsterley, Pontesbury, Hanwood and Bayston Hill (Beistan in the *Chronicles*) before entering the Severn at Shrewsbury. The waters of the brook, which formed the southern boundary of both the abbey precinct and Cadfael's herb garden, were diverted by an artificial stream that not only fed the abbey fish-ponds but also powered the abbey's water-mills. According to the *Twelfth Chronicle (The Raven in the Foregate)*:

> The path on the near side of the mill-pond left the road as a decent cart track, since it had to carry the local corn to the mill, and bring back the flour homeward again. It passed by the three small houses that crowded close to the highway, between their doors and the boundary wall of the abbey, reached the small plateau by the mill, where a wooden bridge crossed the head-race, and thence wandered on as a mere footpath in rough meadow grass by the edge of the water, where several pollarded willows leaned crookedly from the high bank. The first and second cottages were occupied by elderly people who had purchased bed and board for life by the grant of their own property to the abbey. The third belonged to the miller.

The mill and mill-pond lay to the west of the abbey enclave, beyond the high boundary wall, while within stood the great Church of Saint Peter and Saint Paul, together with the monastic buildings, courtyards, gardens and cemetery. Close by the abbey gatehouse was the great west door of the church, the parish door, 'which alone lay outside the precinct wall, and was never closed but in times of great danger and disorder'.* The church building was divided by a stone screen separating the monastic from the secular and 'was equally the parish church of Holy Cross', the nave being open to the people living in the 'relatively law-abiding district' east of the town – the suburb of the Abbey Foregate. Holy Cross was a big parish, with 'a population made up equally of the craftsmen and merchants of the suburb and the cottars and villagers in the countryside'.

*The West door, Shrewsbury Abbey*

'The new priest had only recently been inducted after a lengthy interregnum, and his flock were still carefully taking his measure, after their unhappy experience with the late Father Ailnoth. But first reactions were entirely favourable. Cynric the verger acted as a kind of touchstone for Foregate opinion. His views, so seldom expressed in words, but so easy for the simple and direct to interpret by intuition, would be accepted without question by most of those who worshipped at Holy Cross, and it was already clear to the children, Cynric's closest cronies in spite of his taciturnity, that their long, bony, silent friend liked and approved of Father Boniface. That was enough for them. They approached their new priest with candour and confidence, secure in Cynric's recommendation.

Boniface was young, not much past thirty, of unassuming appearance and modest bearing, no scholar like his predecessor, but earnestly cheerful about his duties. The deference he showed to his monastic neighbours disposed even Prior Robert to approve of him, though with some condescension in view of the young man's humble birth and scanty Latin. Abbot Radulfus, conscious of one disastrous mistake in the previous appointment, had taken his time over this one, and studied the candidates with care. Did the Foregate really need a learned theologian? Craftsmen, small merchants, husbandmen, cottars and hardworking villeins from the villages and manors, they were better off with one of their own kind, aware of their needs and troubles, not stooping to them but climbing laboriously with them, elbow to elbow. It seemed that Father Boniface had energy and determination for the climb, force enough to urge a few others upward with him, and the stubborn loyalty not to leave them behind if they tired. In Latin or in the vernacular, that was language the people could understand.'
The Heretic's Apprentice

* The north door of the abbey church would have also been outside the precinct wall and some authorities argue that this door would have normally been used by parishioners rather than the west door.

*The nave looking east,*
*Shrewsbury Abbey*

*St Paul on west front,*
*Shrewsbury Abbey*

The main orchards and vegetable gardens of the abbey lay to the north, 'not within the precinct, but across the main road, stretched along the rich level beside the river, called the Gaye; and at the far end of this fertile reach there was a slightly higher field' in which crops like corn were grown and sheep were 'turned to graze'. At the end of the field, almost opposite the castle, was an 'old, disused mill', damaged during the siege of 1138.

At the abbey's foundation Earl Roger granted the monks the exclusive right to grind all the town's corn, a right that was confirmed by Henry I. During the next hundred years the citizens of Shrewsbury, who resented the monks' monopoly, began to build their own mills, in violation of the charter. In 1267, in addition to the abbey's mills, there were six horse mills and a windmill, all illegal. When Henry III visited Shrewsbury in the same year the monks appealed and it was agreed that the mills in the suburbs should be destroyed, while those within the town walls and two water-mills on the river were to be owned jointly and the profits shared. It was not until 1328, however, when Edward III granted the town a licence to erect its own mills, that the townspeople were able to grind their corn in complete independence of the abbey.

*'The summer season was at its height, and promising rich harvest, for the spring had been mild and moist after plenteous early snows, and June and July hot and sunny, with a few compensatory showers to keep the leafage fresh and the buds fruitful. The hay harvest was in, and lavish, the corn looked ripe for the sickle. As soon as the annual fair was over, the reaping would begin. Cadfael's fragrant domain, dewy from the dawn and already warming into drunken sweetness in the rising sun, filled his senses with the kind of pleasure on which an ascetic church sometimes frowns, finding something uneasily sinful in pure delight.'* Saint Peter's Fair

In addition to the mills, church, monastic buildings and gardens the abbey maintained a lazarhouse, with adjoining chapel, at the eastern extremity of the Abbey Foregate suburb. Dedicated to Saint Giles, 'patron of the diseased and shunned', the hospital is thought to have been built in the early part of the twelfth century, when leprosy – which had existed in Anglo-Saxon times – was on the increase, perhaps reintroduced into England by the returning crusaders. According to the *Eighth Chronicle (The Devil's Novice)*:

> From the gatehouse to the hospice of Saint Giles was barely half a mile's walk, alongside the enclave wall of the abbey, past the open green of the horsefair, and along the straight road between the houses of the Foregate, until they thinned out with trees and gardens between, and gave place to the open countryside. And there the low roof of the hospital came into view, and the squat tower of its chapel, on a slight rise to the left of the highway, where the road forked.

The buildings, with their wattle-fenced enclosure and 'little, single-aisled church', 'were set discreetly back from both roads that converged towards the town. Lepers, as they may not go among the populous streets of towns, must also keep their distance even to do their begging in the countryside. Saint Giles … had deliberately chosen the desert and the solitary place for his habitation, but these had no choice but to remain apart.'

The number of lepers housed by the hospice at any one time

> varied as the restless wandered on, shunning the town as they must shun all towns, to some other hospice looking over another landscape. By and large, the hospital here sheltered and cared for twenty to thirty inmates at a time. The appointment of the superior rested with the abbey. Brothers and lay brothers served here at their own request. It was not unknown that attendant should become attended, but there was never want of another volunteer to replace and nurse him.

The Church of St Giles,
Shrewsbury

'Beyond the bishop's house the road opened between trees, leaving the
town well behind; and at the fork, a bow-shot ahead, the long, low
roof of the hospice appeared, the wattled fence of its enclosure, and
beyond again, the somewhat higher roof of the church, with a small,
squat turret above. A modest enough church, nave and chancel and
a north aisle, and a graveyard behind, with a carven stone cross set up in the
middle of it. The buildings were set discreetly back from both roads that converged
towards the town. Lepers, as they may not go among the populous streets of the
towns, must also keep their distance even to do their begging in the countryside.
Saint Giles, their patron, had deliberately chosen the desert and the solitary place
for his habitation, but these had no choice but to remain apart.'

*The Leper of Saint Giles*

*The north aisle, chancel, nave and south side of St Giles' Church*

*The exact date of the foundation of St Giles is uncertain, but it is thought to have been built during the early twelfth century. Some authorities, however, claim that it was founded by Roger de Montgomery in the late eleventh century. It is known that the Church of St Giles formed part of a hospital for lepers in the reign of Henry II. Up until 1857, when it became a separate parish, St Giles was part of the parish of Holy Cross and until the Dissolution it was almost certainly served by one of the monks from Shrewsbury Abbey. In the early eighteenth century the church was in a bad state of repair and in the following century it was extensively restored and enlarged: alterations which included the rebuilding of the north aisle, the lengthening of the nave, the construction of the north transept and the building of a new chancel. The church was re-opened in 1895. No trace of the hospital now survives. The oldest parts of the present church building are the south wall and doorway, built of red sandstone and dating from the early twelfth century or possibly earlier. The wooden porch was built in 1858.*

Cadfael, who 'visited Saint Giles every third week, and sometimes oftener, to replenish the medicine cupboard', had

> done his year or more in this labour, and felt no recoil, and only measured pity, respect being so much greater an encouragement and support. Moreover, he came and went here so regularly that his visits were a part of a patient and permanent routine like the services in the church. He had dressed more and viler sores than he troubled to remember, and discovered live hearts and vigorous minds within the mottled shells he tended. He had seen battles, too, in his time in the world, as far afield as Acre and Ascalon and Jerusalem in the first Crusade, and witnessed deaths crueller than disease, and heathen kinder than Christians, and he knew of leprosies of the heart and ulcers of the soul worse than any of these he poulticed and lanced with his herbal medicines.

The Abbey of Saint Peter and Saint Paul at Shrewsbury flourished and prospered for nearly five hundred years, until 1540, when, by order of Henry VIII, it was dissolved and many of the monastic buildings were destroyed. At the time of its dissolution the monastery held twenty-six manors in Shropshire, land in the counties of Yorkshire, Staffordshire and Cheshire, and the priory of Saint Bartholomew in Smithfield, London. The abbey church, originally 302 feet from east to west and 133 feet across the transepts, was demolished, except for the nave and western tower, which served as the parish church of the Holy Cross. A wall was built between the pillars at the eastern end and, in the mid-1880s, the church was restored and extended eastward (though not to its original size) to create the present Choir and Lady Chapel.

The few remaining monastic buildings, having survived the Dissolution and escaped major damage during the English Civil War, were demolished in 1836 when Thomas Telford constructed his new road linking London to Holyhead. In the process, he created a new and straighter Abbey Foregate immediately to the south of the church, through where the cloisters would have been. The rest of the site was destroyed in the mid-nineteenth century to make way for the railway, with its station, depots and sidings sprawling across much of the former abbey grounds. Yet, despite this widespread clearance and development to the east of the town, one structure – apart from the present abbey church and parts of what may have been the infirmary – managed, remarkably, to survive: the Refectory Pulpit.

This unique, hooded, octagonal stone structure still stands in its original position (now near a railway siding) and is all that remains of the medieval monastic refectory or common dining-room. From this indoor pulpit, as the monks ate their meal in silence, one of the brothers would read aloud passages celebrating the lives of the saints. In the *First Chronicle (A Morbid Taste For Bones)* Brother John, once Cadfael's assistant in the garden, took a turn as reader 'and however dull the passage they chose for him in the refectory, and innocuous the saints and martyrs he would have to celebrate at chapter, John would contrive to imbue them with drama and gusto from his own sources. Give him the beheading of Saint John the Baptist, and he would shake the foundations.'

Although the refectory is thought to have been Norman, the pulpit was built much later, probably towards the end of the fourteenth century when Nicholas Stevens was Abbot (1361–99). Today it no longer faces into the medieval refectory but into a small, railed shrub garden, situated to the south of the abbey church and across the main road. Amongst its fine stone carvings, now sadly eroded, are three panels: in the centre a representation of the Annunciation; on the right the figures of Saint Peter and Saint Paul; and on the left, Saint Winifred and Saint Beuno. Inside the vaulted roof, on the central boss, is a well-preserved carving representing the Crucifixion with the Virgin Mary and Saint John standing at the foot of the cross.

The *Tenth Chronicle (The Pilgrim of Hate)* records that in the summer of 1141 the monastery had fifty-three brothers, seven novices and six schoolboys, 'as well as all the lay stewards and servants'.* Brother Cadfael, 'who had roamed the world from Wales to Jerusalem and back to Normandy for forty years before committing himself to stability within the cloister', was amongst them. One evening, after supper, he emerged from the refectory, having listened to readings from Saint Augustine, and looked upon the great Benedictine abbey of Shrewsbury, his 'whole small world', 'from the roses in the garden to the wrought stones of the cloister walls, and found it unquestionably beautiful'.

---

* Although the *Chronicles of Brother Cadfael* refer to fifty-three brothers, records suggest that there were never more than nineteen.

*Refectory Pulpit, Shrewsbury Abbey*

'Brother Cadfael on his way to the refectory saw Aelfric crossing the great court from the abbot's kitchen, heading quickly for the gatehouse, bearing before him a high-rimmed wooden tray laden with covered dishes. Guests enjoyed a more relaxed diet than the brothers, though it did not differ greatly except in the amount of meat, and at this time of year that would already be salt beef. To judge by the aroma that wafted from the tray as it passed, beef boiled with onions, and served with a dish of beans. The small covered bowl balanced on top had a much more appetising smell. Evidently the newcomer was to enjoy an intermissum today, before coming to the apples from the orchard . . .

'Cadfael went on to the refectory, and his own dinner, which turned out to be boiled beef and beans, as he had foreseen. No savoury intermissum here.'

*Monk's Hood*

*Crucifixion on boss, Refectory Pulpit, Shrewsbury Abbey*

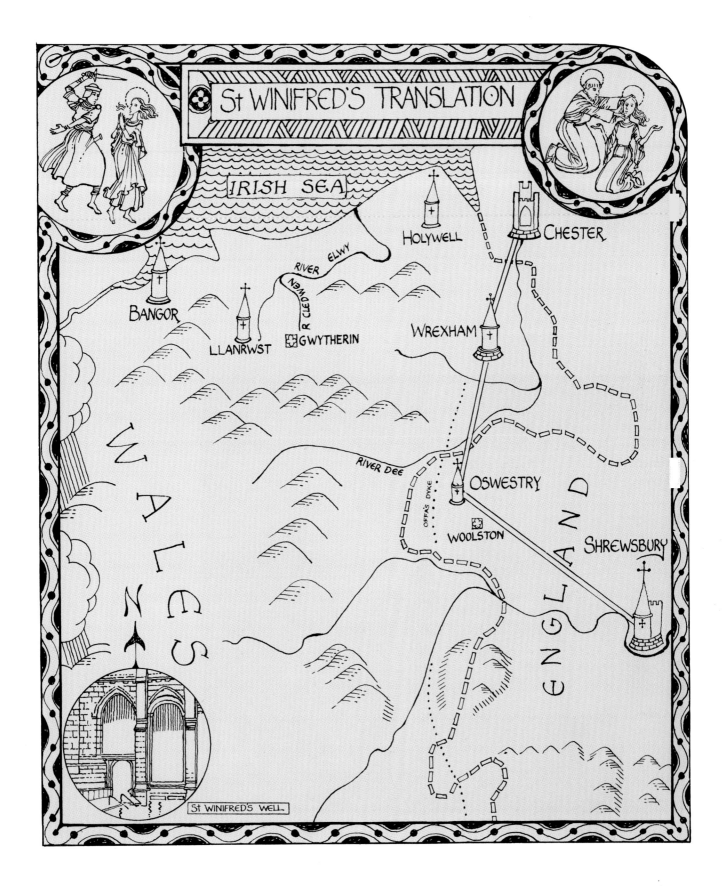

# St WINIFRED'S TRANSLATION

IRISH SEA

HOLYWELL

CHESTER

RIVER ELWY

R CLEDWEN

BANGOR

LLANRWST

GWYTHERIN

WREXHAM

WALES

RIVER DEE

OSWESTRY

OFFA'S DYKE

WOOLSTON

ENGLAND

SHREWSBURY

N

St WINIFRED'S WELL

# Saint Winifred

I n a remote Welsh mountain valley, almost five miles directly east of Llanrwst (Gwynedd), lies the village of Gwytherin in the county of Clwyd, the burial place of Saint Winifred and the objective of an expedition taken by the Benedictine monks of Shrewsbury in 1137* to acquire her sacred bones for their monastery. Although the *First Chronicle of Brother Cadfael (A Morbid Taste for Bones)* is based on this historical journey, the events and monastic characters depicted in it – except Prior Robert Pennant and Abbot Heribert – are entirely fictional.

When the expedition returned to the Abbey of Saint Peter and Saint Paul at Shrewsbury, according to the *Chronicle*, all but Brother Cadfael were confident that they had triumphed in their mission. He, however, knew otherwise, having gone to great pains to conceal from Prior Robert and his fellow brothers the 'truth' about certain happenings at Gwytherin. He felt strongly that he had no alternative, for had the 'truth' been revealed, it would have brought a 'fearful scandal … to smirch the abbey of Shrewsbury, and all the force of the Benedictine Order'. How could he reveal that it was not Saint Winifred they had brought back from Wales in their 'resplendent coffin' but the body of Brother Columbanus, who in ignorance they thought had been miraculously 'taken up living out of this world'?

Saint Winifred, says the *Chronicle*,

was the only child of a knight named Tevyth, who lived in those parts when the princes were yet heathens. But this knight and all his household were converted by Saint Beuno, and made him a church there, and gave him house-room. The girl was devoted even above her parents, and pledged herself to a virgin life, hearing Mass

---

*Some histories give the year of Saint Winifred's translation as 1138, not 1137. Prior Robert Pennant's book states that the expedition took place 'in the second regnal year of King Stephen'. As Stephen was anointed King on 22 December 1135, his second year begins on 22 December 1136, making the May journey definitely 1137.

every day. But one Sunday it happened that she was sick, and stayed at home when all the rest of the household went to church. And there came to the door the prince of those parts, Cradoc, son of the king, who had fallen in love with her at a distance. For this girl was very beautiful.

Pleading 'that he was hot and parched from hunting', he 'asked for a drink of water, and the girl let him in and gave him to drink'. Once inside, he 'pressed his suit upon her, and grappled her in his arms'. The 'faithful virgin put him off with soft words, and escaping into another room, climbed from a window and fled towards the church. But finding that she had eluded him, Prince Cradoc took horse and rode after, and overtaking her just within sight of the church, and dreading that she would reveal his infamy, struck off her head with his sword.' At that moment,

> Saint Beuno and the congregation were coming out of the church, and saw what had passed. The saint drew a terrible curse upon the murderer, who at once sank to the ground, and began to melt like wax in a fire, until all his body had sunk away into the grass. Then Saint Beuno fitted the head of the virgin onto her neck, and the flesh grew together, and she stood up alive, and the holy fountain sprang up on the spot where she arose.

The place where this miraculous fountain of water sprang up became known as Treffynnon in Welsh and Holywell in English.

Later, Saint Winifred went on a pilgrimage to Rome, 'and she attended at a great synod of saints, and was appointed to be prioress over a community of virgin sisters at Gwytherin, by Llanrwst. And there she lived many years, and did many miracles in her lifetime.'

*St Winifred (also spelled Winefride and known as Gwenfrewi in Welsh) lived in the seventh century, almost certainly at Holywell (Treffynnon) in North Wales. One legend says that, after Prince Caradoc had cut off her head with his sword, it rolled down the hillside and where it came to rest a fountain of pure water gushed out of the ground. Holywell became a great centre of pilgrimage and the water from the well was famed for its miraculous healing properties. The present chapel which encloses the well was built at the end of the fifteenth century. It was drastically altered from the eighteenth century onwards and only recently restored. The water was cut off in 1917 when mining operations at Halkyn diverted the underground stream and although the supply of water was connected to another source, the flow is now much reduced.*

*St Winefride's Well,
Holywell, Clwyd*

*The Church of St Winifred,*
*Gwytherin, Clwyd*

She was buried in the churchyard at Gwytherin, overlooking the valley of the Afon Cledwen, a tributary of the Elwy which joins the Clwyd near Llanelwy (St Asaph). Her bones remained undisturbed at Gwytherin for almost five hundred years, until Prior Robert, envious of the Cluniac priory of Wenlock, 'a few miles distant, with its own miracle-working saint', decided to find 'a spare saint' for the Benedictine abbey of Shrewsbury and – seemingly through divine guidance – was directed to Winifred.

The events, as described in the *First Chronicle*, are as follows. One May morning in the year 1137 Brother Columbanus, a young Benedictine monk of Shrewsbury, 'barely a year tonsured' and coming from a 'formidable, aristocratic Norman family, a younger son despatched to make his way in the monastic ranks as next-best to inheriting land', fell to the floor of the chapter-house, overcome by some kind of fit. Many of the brothers 'hovered in helpless shock' as the young man 'lay on his face, threshing and jerking like a landed fish, beating his forehead and his palms against the flagstones, kicking and flailing with long, pale legs bared to the knee by his contortions, and barking out of him those extraordinary sounds of shattering physical excitement'. Eventually Columbanus was overpowered and, after being securely bound and gagged to prevent him from hurting himself, he was carried to the infirmary, where he was subdued by a draught of Brother Cadfael's 'poppy-juice'. Prior Robert instructed his 'faithful hound', 'toady and shadow', Brother Jerome, to sit constantly by the young man's bedside day and night to watch over him, in case the fit should come again.

Brother Jerome appeared at chapter next morning with an exalted countenance, and the air of one bursting with momentous news. At Abbot Heribert's mild reproof for leaving his patient without permission, he folded his hands meekly and bowed his head, but lost none of his rapt assurance.

'Father, I am sent here by another duty, that seemed to me even more urgent. I have left Brother Columbanus sleeping, though not peacefully, for even his sleep is tormented. But two lay-brothers are watching by him. If I have done wrong, I will abide it humbly.'

'Our brother is no better?' asked the abbot anxiously.

'He is still deeply troubled, and when he wakes he raves. But Father, this is my errand! There is a sure hope for him! In the night I have been miraculously visited. I have come to tell you what divine mercy has instructed me. Father, in the small hours I fell into a doze beside Brother Columbanus' bed, and had a marvellous sweet dream.'

'Father,' Jerome continued, 'it seemed to me that the wall of the room opened, and a great light shone in, and through the light and radiating the light there came in a most beautiful young virgin, and stood beside our brother's bed, and spoke to me. She told me that her name was Winifred, and that in Wales there is a holy spring, that rose to the light where she suffered martyrdom. And she said that if Brother

Columbanus bathed in the water of that well, he would surely be healed, and restored at once to his senses. Then she uttered a blessing upon our house, and vanished in a great light, and I awoke.'

Through the murmur of excitement that went round the chapter-house, Prior Robert's voice rose in reverent triumph: 'Father Abbot, we are being guided! Our quest for a saint has drawn to us this sign of favour, in token that we should persevere.'

And persevere they did. With the blessing and prayers of the Abbot, Brother Columbanus was escorted to Holywell, a village located across the border in Clwyd, North Wales, two days distant, where he was immersed in the sacred waters of Saint Winifred's spring and instantly healed. Jerome, who witnessed the 'miracle', brought back encouraging news, confirming the whereabouts of the virgin's bones:

> 'And, Father,' he duly reported to the abbot, 'the people there told us that the saint is indeed buried at Gwytherin, where she died after her ministry, and that the place where her body is laid has done many miracles. But they say that her tomb, after so long, is neglected and little thought of, and it may well be that she longs for a better recognition, and to be installed in some place where pilgrims may come, where she may be revered as is her due, and have room to enlarge her grace and blessing to reach more people in need.'
>
> 'You are inspired, having been present at this miracle,' said Prior Robert, tall and splendid with faith rewarded, 'and you speak out what I have felt in listening to you. Surely Saint Winifred is calling us to her rescue as she came to the rescue of Brother Columbanus. Many have need of her goodness as he had, and know nothing of her. In our hands she would be exalted as she deserves, and those who need her grace would know where to come and seek it. I pray that we may mount that expedition of faith to which she summons us. Father Abbot, give me your leave to petition the church, and bring this blessed lady home to rest here among us, and be our proudest boast. For I believe it is her will and her command.'
>
> 'In the name of God,' said Abbot Heribert devoutly, 'I approve that project, and pray the blessing of heaven upon it!'

Later that same May day, Cadfael and his 'cheerful, blunt, extrovert' assistant, Brother John, were working in the herb garden. Prior Robert

> 'had it all planned beforehand,' said Brother John over the bed of mint, between envy and scorn. 'That was all a show, all that wonder and amazement, and asking who Saint Winifred was, and where to find her. He knew it all along. He'd already picked her out from those he's discovered neglected in Wales, and decided she was the one most likely to be available, as well as the one to shed most lustre on him. But it had to come out into the open by miraculous means. There'll be another prodigy whenever he needs his way smoothed for him, until he gets the girl here safely installed in the church, to his glory. It's a great enterprise, he means to climb high on the strength of

*The statue of St Winefride, depicting the saint as an abbess carrying a crook, was placed in the niche above the well in 1888. The palm leaf signifies her martyrdom and the thin line around her neck shows where her head was severed from her body before being miraculously restored*

it. So he starts out with a vision, and a prodigious healing, and divine grace leading his footsteps. It's as plain as the nose on your face.'

'And are you saying,' asked Brother Cadfael mildly, 'that Brother Columbanus is in the plot as well as Brother Jerome, and that falling fit of his was a fake, too? I should be very sure of my reward in heaven before I volunteered to break the paving with my forehead, even to provide Prior Robert with a miracle.'

Brother John considered seriously, frowning. 'No, that I don't say. We all know our meek white lamb is liable to the horrors over a penance scamped, and ecstasies over a vigil or a fast, and pouring ice-cold water over him at Holywell would be the very treatment to jolt him back into his right wits. We could just as well have tossed him in the fish-pond here! But of course he'd believe what they told him, and credit it all to the saint. Catch him missing such a chance! No, I wouldn't say he was a party to it – not knowingly. But he gave them the opportunity for a splendid demonstration of grace. You notice it was Jerome who was set to take care of him overnight! It takes only one man to be favoured with a vision, but it has to be the right man.' He rolled a sprig of the young green leaves sadly between his palms, and the fragrance distilled richly on the early morning air. 'And it will be the right men who'll accompany Prior Robert into Wales,' he said with sour certainty. 'You'll see!'

No doubt about it, this young man was hankering after a glimpse of the world again, and a breath of air from outside the walls, Brother Cadfael pondered, not only with sympathy for his young assistant, but also with some pleasurable stirrings of his own. So momentous an event in the otherwise even course of monastic life ought not to be missed. Besides the undoubted possibilities of mischief!

'True!' he said thoughtfully. 'Perhaps we ought to take some steps to leaven the lump. Wales should not be left with the notion that Jerome is the best Shrewsbury can muster, that's very true.'

'You have about as much chance of being invited as I,' said Brother John with his customary bluntness. 'Jerome is sure of his place, Prior Robert must have his right hand with him. And Columbanus, fool innocent, was the instrument of grace, and could be made to serve the same turn again. Brother Sub-Prior they have to take along, for form's sake. Surely we could think up some way of getting a foot in the door? They can't move for a few days yet, the carpenters and carvers are working hard on this splendid reliquary coffin they're going to take with them for the lady, but it will take them a while to finish it. Get your wits to work, brother! There isn't anything you couldn't do, if you've a mind! Prior or no prior!'

'Well, well, did I say you had not faith?' wondered Brother Cadfael, charmed and disarmed. 'I might worm my way in, there could be ways, but how am I to recommend a graceless rogue like you? What are you good at, to be taken along on such an errand?'

'I'm a good hand with mules,' said Brother John hopefully, 'and you don't think Prior Robert intends to go on foot, I suppose? Or to do the grooming and feeding and watering himself? Or the mucking-out? They'll need somebody to do the hard work, and wait on them. Why not me?'

*Chapel of St Winefride,
Holywell, Clwyd*

*St Winefride's Well, together with the parish church at Holywell, belonged to the
Cistercian monks of Basingwerk Abbey from 1240 until the Dissolution. The
Church of St James, on the opposite side of the road to the well, stands on the same
site as the seventh-century chapel, built of wood by St Beuno. The Countess
Adeliza of Chester gave the church, probably then built of stone, to the Benedictine
Abbey of St Werburgh at Chester in 1093. By the end of the fifteenth century the
parish church was rebuilt, except for the west tower, and the present chapel
enclosing the well was constructed in Perpendicular style. The Chapel of St
Winefride was probably built under the patronage of Lady Margaret, Countess of
Richmond, mother of Henry VII. It was a major centre of pilgrimage until the
Reformation, when measures were taken to inhibit people from visiting the sacred
waters. Today, the well is still a place of pilgrimage and is called the Lourdes of
Wales.*

Why not indeed? After dinner Brother Cadfael sought out Abbot Heribert in his study.

'Father Abbot, it is on my mind that we are undertaking this pilgrimage to Gwytherin without full consideration. First we must send to the bishop of Bangor, in whose see Gwytherin lies, for without his approval the matter cannot proceed. Now it is not essential to have a speaker fluent in Welsh there, since the bishop is obviously conversant with Latin. But not every parish priest in Wales has that tongue, and it is vital to be able to speak freely with the priest at Gwytherin, should the bishop sanction our quest. But most of all, the see of Bangor is wholly within the sovereignty of the king of Gwynedd, and surely his goodwill and permission are essential as those of the church. The princes of Gwynedd speak only in Welsh, though they have learned clerks. Father Prior, certainly, has a smattering of Welsh, but ...'

'That is very true,' said Abbot Heribert, easily dismayed. 'It is but a smattering. And the king's agreement is all-important. Brother Cadfael, Welsh is your first, best language, and has no mysteries for you. Could *you* ...? The garden, I am aware ... But with your aid there would be no problem.'

'In the garden,' said Brother Cadfael, 'everything is well forward, and can manage without me ten days or more, and take no hurt. I should be glad indeed to be the interpreter, and lend my skills also in Gwytherin.'

'Then so be it!' sighed the abbot in heartfelt relief. 'Go with Prior Robert, and be our voice to the Welsh people. I shall sanction your errand myself, and you will have my authority.'

He was old and human and gentle, full of experience, short on ambition, self-righteousness and resolution. There could have been two ways of approaching him concerning Brother John. Cadfael took the more honest and simple way.

'Father, there is a young brother concerning whose vocation I have doubts, but concerning whose goodness I have none. He is close to me, and I would that he might find his true way, for if he finds it he will not forsake it. But it may not be with us. I beg that I may take him with me, as our hewer of wood and drawer of water in this enterprise, to allow him time to consider.'

The Abbot, although 'faintly dismayed and apprehensive', proved to be sympathetic to Cadfael's request and permission was granted. The inclusion of Cadfael and Brother John in the expedition swelled the number to six, the other four being Prior Robert, Sub-Prior Richard, Brother Jerome and Brother Columbanus.

They set out from Shrewsbury as soon as 'the fine reliquary for the saint's bones was ready, polished oak ornamented with silver, to serve as a proof what honours awaited Winifred in her new shrine', and arrived in Bangor in the third week of May. Bishop David and Prince Owain, 'who was the regent of Gwynedd', both readily agreed to the proposed translation and, 'episcopally and royally blessed', Prior Robert's party set off for Gwytherin, confident of a 'triumphant end'.

They turned aside from the Conway valley at Llanrwst, climbing away from the river into forested country. Beyond the watershed they crossed the Elwy where it is young and small, and moved steadily south-eastwards through thick woods, over another ridge of high land, to descend once again into the upland valley of a little river, that provided some marshy water-meadows along its banks, and a narrow band of tilled fields, sloping and sturdy but protected by the forests above these lush pastures. The wooded ridge on either hand ran in oblique folds, richly green, hiding the scattered house-steads. The fields were already planted, and here and there orchards flowered. Below them, there was a small stone church, whitewashed and shimmering, and a little wooden house beside it.

'You see the goal of your pilgrimage,' said the chaplain Urien [who had been sent by Prince Owain to be their guide]. He was a compact, neat, well-shaven personage, handsomely dressed and mounted, more of an ambassador than a clerk.

'That is Gwytherin?' asked Prior Robert.

'It is the church and priest's house of Gwytherin. The parish stretches for several miles along the river valley, and a mile or more from the Cledwen on either bank. We do not congregate in villages as you English do. Land good for hunting is plentiful, but good for tillage meagre. Every man lives where best suits him for working his fields and conserving his game.'

'It is a very fair place,' said the sub-prior, and meant it, for the fold on fold of well-treed hills beyond the river made a pattern of spring beauty in a hundred different greens, and the water-meadows were strung like a necklace of emeralds along the fringes of a necklace of silver and lapis-lazuli.

Across the river, some way below them and a great way off, the snaky curve of the furrows already patterned the slope between cultivated fields and leaning trees, a dark brown writing upon the hillside, and on the higher furrow, as yet uncompleted, the oxen leaned into their yokes and heaved, and the ploughman behind them clung and dragged at the heavy share. Before the leading pair a man walked backwards, arms gently waving and beckoning, his goad only a wand, flourished for magic, not for its sting, his high, pure calls carried aloft on the air, cajoling and praising. Towards him the beasts leaned willingly, following his cries with all their might. The new-turned soil, greyish-brown and sluggish, heaved moist and fresh to light after the share.

'A harsh country,' said Urien, as one assessing, not complaining, and set his horse moving downhill towards the church. 'Come, I'll hand you over to Father Huw, and see you well-received.'

Father Huw, the parish priest, welcomed the Benedictine delegation from Shrewsbury but, although they came with the blessing of the Welsh Prince and also the Bishop, he warned them that the people of Gwytherin were not going to like their saint being 'dug up out of her grave and taken away into England'.

After severe opposition from the local Welsh inhabitants, Prior Robert eventually 'succeeded' in his mission and returned to the Abbey of Saint Peter and Saint Paul with what everyone – except Cadfael – thought were the bones of Saint Winifred.

*Woods near Gwytherin, Clwyd*

*Hills above Gwytherin*

It was not until four years later, in the *Tenth Chronicle (The Pilgrim of Hate)*, that Cadfael finally confided to his close friend, Hugh Beringar of Maesbury, Sheriff of Shropshire, the truth about what had happened in Gwytherin – a secret that both friends took for granted would be safely kept between them.

'There was one Welsh lord of Gwytherin,' said Cadfael, 'who would not suffer the girl to be disturbed, and would not be persuaded or bribed or threatened into letting her go. And he died, Hugh – murdered. By one of us, a brother who came from high rank, and had his eyes already set on a mitre. And when we came near to accusing him, it was his life or a better. There were certain young people of that place put in peril by him, the dead lord's daughter and her lover. The boy lashed out in anger, with good reason, seeing his girl wounded and bleeding. He was stronger than he knew. The murderer's neck was broken.'

'How many knew of this?' asked Hugh, his eyes narrowed thoughtfully upon the glossy-leaved rose-bushes.

'When it befell, only the lovers, the dead man and I. And Saint Winifred, who had been raised from her grave and laid in that casket of which you and all men know. She knew. She was there. From the moment I raised her,' said Cadfael, 'and by God, it was I who took her from the soil, and I who restored her – and still that makes me glad – from the moment I uncovered those slender bones, I felt in mine they wished only to be left in peace. It was so little and so wild and quiet a graveyard there, with the small church long out of use, meadow flowers growing over all, and the mounds so modest and green. And Welsh soil! The girl was Welsh, like me, her church was of the old persuasion, what did she know of this alien English shire? And I had those young things to keep. Who would have taken their word or mine against all the force of the church? They would have closed their ranks to bury the scandal, and bury the boy with it, and he guilty of nothing but defending his dear. So I took measures.'

Hugh's mobile lips twitched. 'Now indeed you amaze me! And what measures were those? With a dead brother to account for, and Prior Robert to keep sweet ...'

'Ah, well, Robert is a simpler soul than he supposes, and then I had a good deal of help from the dead brother himself. He'd been busy building himself such a reputation for sanctity, delivering messages from the saint herself – it was he told us she was offering the grave she'd left to the murdered man – and going into trance-sleeps, and praying to leave this world and be taken into bliss living ... So we did him that small favour. He'd been keeping a solitary night-watch in the old church, and in the morning when it ended, there were his habit and sandals fallen together at his prayer-stool, and the body of him lifted clean out of them, in sweet odours and a shower of may-blossom. That was how he claimed the saint had already visited him, why should not Robert recall it and believe? Certainly he was gone. Why look for him? Would a modest brother of our house be running through the Welsh woods mother-naked?'

'Are you telling me,' asked Hugh cautiously, 'that what you have there in the reliquary is *not* ... Then the casket had not yet been sealed?' His eyebrows were tangling with his black forelock, but his voice was soft and unsurprised.

'Well ...' Cadfael twitched his blunt brown nose bashfully between finger and thumb. 'Sealed it was, but there are ways of dealing with seals that leave them unblemished. It's one of the more dubious of my remembered skills, but for all that I was glad of it then.'

'And you put the lady back in the place that was hers, along with her champion?'

'He was a decent, good man, and had spoken up for her nobly. She would not grudge him house-room. I have always thought,' confided Cadfael, 'that she was not displeased with us. She has shown her power in Gwytherin since that time, by many miracles, so I cannot believe she is angry. But what a little troubles me is that she has not so far chosen to favour us with any great mark of her patronage here, to keep Robert happy, and set my mind at rest.'

*St Winifred's Well, Woolston*

*Thirteen miles north-west of Shrewsbury and four miles south-east of Oswestry is the hamlet of Woolston, once a place of pilgrimage. It is reputed that, while the relics of St Winifred were being carried from North Wales to Shrewsbury in 1137, a spring miraculously appeared at Woolston on the spot where the saint's reliquary was put down to rest. Today the spring, which still flows, is housed beneath the projecting gabled porch of a timber-framed cottage, built about 400 years ago as a courthouse. The water in the well is reputed to heal wounds, bruises and fractured bones, while the small spring below is alleged to relieve sore eyes*

Yet, despite his misgivings, Cadfael, even then, did not see what else he could have done.

'It was an ending that satisfied everyone,' he confessed, 'both here and there. The children were free to marry and be happy, the village still had its saint, and she had her own people around her. Robert had what he had gone to find – or thought he had, which is the same thing. And Shrewsbury abbey has its festival, with every hope of a full guest-hall, and glory and gain in good measure ...'

'And you've never said word of this to anyone?'

'Never a word. But the whole village of Gwytherin knows it,' admitted Cadfael with a remembering grin. 'No one told, no one had to tell, but they knew. There wasn't a man missing when we took up the reliquary and set out for home. They helped to carry it, whipped together a little chariot to bear it. Robert thought he had them nicely tamed, even those who'd been most reluctant from the first. It was a great joy to him. A simple soul at bottom! It would be great pity to undo him now, when he's busy writing his book about the saint's life, and how he brought her to Shrewsbury.'

The historical facts are that Prior Robert Pennant really did write a book about the life of Saint Winifred, completing it with an account of the translation of her bones from Gwytherin to England. As most of the events in the *First Chronicle* are fictitious, there is, of course, no mention in his record of Brother Columbanus's body, or indeed any other, being substituted for the saint's bones; nor for that matter is there any mention of a brother named Cadfael. That omission, however, Cadfael himself had confidently predicted!

The relics of Saint Winifred remained in the abbey at Shrewsbury for a further four hundred years, until the dissolution of the monastery in 1540, when her shrine was demolished and her bones disappeared. Parts of her shrine were discovered in 1933 in a Shrewsbury garden and were returned to the abbey. Today Saint Winifred has a small shrine in the nave, where there is an ancient stone bearing three carved figures: Saint Winifred in the centre, flanked by Saint Beuno, her uncle, on the right and Saint John the Baptist on the left. One of her finger-bones found its way to Rome and was returned to England in 1852, where it was divided in two, 'one half being sent to Holywell and the other to Shrewsbury where presumably it still exists'.

As a place of pilgrimage, Shrewsbury ranked second only to the shrine of Saint Thomas at Canterbury. In 1487 Abbot Thomas Mynde, by payment of 'a great sum of money to the royal coffers' (Forrest), obtained a licence from Henry VII to found the 'Guild of Saint Winefride'. Five centuries later, in 1987, the Guild was revived by the Friends of the Abbey; according to the notes adjacent to her shrine, Saint Winifred's cult is the only one in England to have persisted to the present day.

*St Winifred flanked by St Beuno and St John the Baptist, St Winifred's Shrine, Shrewsbury Abbey*

'After dinner, in the half-hour or so allowed for rest, Cadfael went into the church, into the grateful stony coolness, and stood for some minutes silent before St Winifred's altar. Of late, if he felt the need to speak to her in actual words at all, he found himself addressing her in Welsh, but usually he relied on her to know all the preoccupations of his mind without words. Doubtful, in any case, if the young and beautiful Welsh girl of her first brief life had known any English or Latin, or even been able to read and write her own language, though the stately prioress of her second life, pilgrim to Rome and head of a community of holy women, must have had time to learn and study to her heart's content. But it was as the girl that Cadfael always imagined her. A girl whose beauty was legendary, and caused her to be coveted by princes.'

*The Heretic's Apprentice*

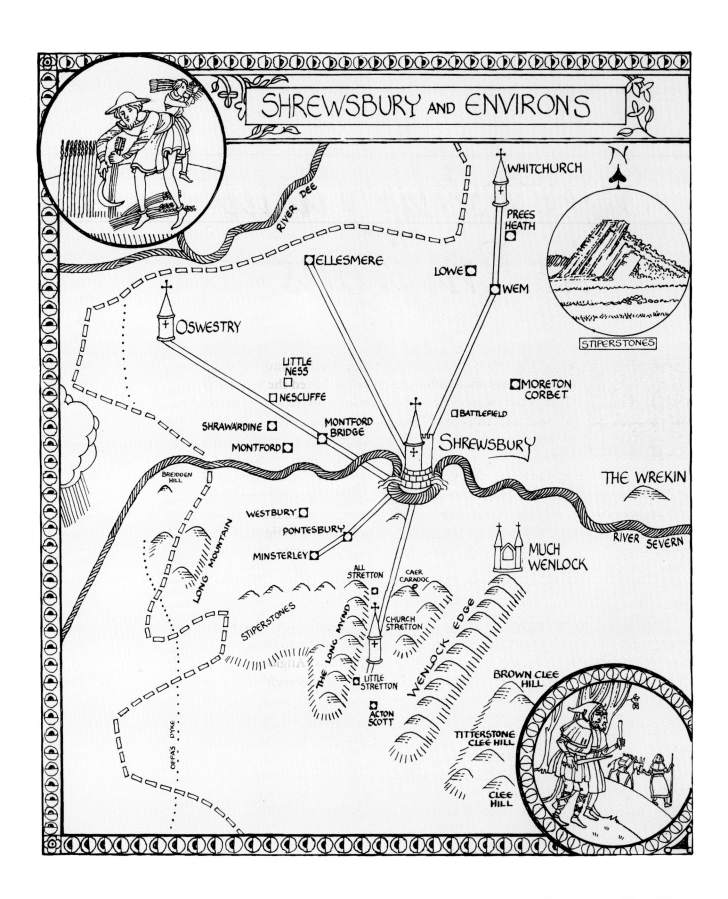

# SHREWSBURY AND ENVIRONS

RIVER DEE

WHITCHURCH

PREES HEATH

ELLESMERE

LOWE

WEM

STIPERSTONES

OSWESTRY

LITTLE NESS

MORETON CORBET

NESCLIFFE

BATTLEFIELD

SHRAWARDINE

MONTFORD BRIDGE

SHREWSBURY

MONTFORD

THE WREKIN

BREIDDEN HILL

WESTBURY

RIVER SEVERN

PONTESBURY

MINSTERLEY

MUCH WENLOCK

LONG MOUNTAIN

ALL STRETTON

CAER CARADOC

STIPERSTONES

CHURCH STRETTON

WENLOCK EDGE

THE LONG MYND

BROWN CLEE HILL

LITTLE STRETTON

ACTON SCOTT

TITTERSTONE CLEE HILL

OFFA'S DYKE

CLEE HILL

# Shrewsbury and its Environs

amed after the ancient town of Shrewsbury, Shropshire did not exist until the tenth century, when Alfred the Great and his successors divided the country into administrative shires (a word derived from the Anglo-Saxon *scir*, meaning 'sphere of office'). Each shire was administered from a fortified centre – Shrewsbury, in the case of Shropshire – and was run by the king's direct representative, the sheriff or 'shire-reeve', under an ealdorman or earl. The first mention of the Anglo-Saxon shire of Scrobbescire or Shropshire is in *The Anglo-Saxon Chronicle* when, in the year 1006, King Ethelred the Unready, pursued by the Danes, 'passed over the Thames into Scrobbes-byrig-scire' and spent Christmas in Shrewsbury. The Normans called the county Salopescire (Salop) and the county town Salopesbiry (Shrewsbury or simply Salop). Both forms are still in use today, although the Anglo-Saxon name of Shropshire is the most popular.

Shropshire is a border county and throughout its early history was of strategic importance in the age-old conflict between the native hill people to the west and the invading peoples from the east, whether Celts, Romans, Anglo-Saxons or Normans. In the twelfth century (the period in which *The Chronicles of Brother Cadfael* are set) the Celtic Welsh, particularly the men of Powys, made frequent incursions across the border into England, taking advantage of the fact that the Normans were preoccupied with the long fratricidal civil war between King Stephen and his cousin the Empress Maud.

Indeed, despite the fact that the Normans built numerous fortifications along the border, they were unable to stop the Welsh from making gains in Shropshire. Madog ap Meredith, Prince of Powys, for example, ruled over the

*Nesscliffe Hill*

*The red sandstone cliffs of the wooded Nesscliffe Hill lie immediately to the east of the main Shrewsbury to Oswestry road, with the village of Nesscliffe straddling the highway. The hill has been quarried for its building stone for centuries and on its summit are the earthwork remains of two Iron Age forts. At the southern end of the hill is a cave, cut out of the solid rock; this was reputedly the hideout of Humphrey Kynaston who was outlawed in 1491 and has been called Shropshire's Robin Hood. He died in 1534*

Lordship of Oswestry in the north-west of the shire from 1149 to 1157. Long after the accession of Henry II, when FitzAlan regained possession of the castle, Oswestry was sacked and burnt on several occasions, sometimes by the Welsh and sometimes by the English. It was not until 1536, when the Act of Union of England and Wales was passed, that the town became an integral part of England and was placed firmly and officially in Shropshire.

Before peace finally triumphed in the mid-seventeenth century the county suffered not only from innumerable local skirmishes but also from major wars. These included the battles between King John and Llywelyn the Great (1173–1240), grandson of Owain Gwynedd, which continued well into the reign of Henry III, and the Battle of Shrewsbury. This latter took place north of the town on 21 July 1403, when Henry IV and his young son, Prince Hal of Shakespeare's *Henry IV Part II* and later Henry V, defeated and killed Sir Henry Percy, known as Hotspur.

Geographically and geologically, Shropshire is divided almost equally in two by the meandering course of the River Severn, with lowlands to the north and east and uplands to the south. There are anomalies, however, to this simplification: the volcanic hog-back of the Wrekin, for example, lies to the north of the river and rises abruptly from the Shropshire plain like some giant sleeping prehistoric reptile. Isolated sandstone hills such as Nesscliffe and Grinshill can also be found in the north and many have been quarried for their building stone. Grinshill stone in particular is well known for its fine quality and has been used both for buildings throughout the county and for many of the churches, bridges and larger buildings of Shrewsbury.

*River Severn, near Atcham*

In the extreme north-west of Shropshire the market town of Oswestry nestles in the foothills of Wales above the Shropshire plain. Hugh Beringar, according to the *Eleventh Chronicle (An Excellent Mystery),*

was a man of the northern part of the shire himself, but from the Welsh border; and the manors to the north-east, dwindling into the plain of Cheshire, were less familiar to him and less congenial. Over in the tamer country of the hundred of Hodnet the soil was fat and well-farmed, and the gleaned grain-fields full of plump, contented cattle at graze, at once making good use of what aftermath there was in a dry season, and leaving their droppings to feed the following year's tilth. There were abbey tenants here and there in these parts, and abbey stock turned into the fields now the crop was reaped. Their treading and manuring of the ground was almost as valuable as their fleeces.

The *Eighth Chronicle (The Devil's Novice)* observes that, between Hodnet and Oswestry, 'in the north of the shire the land was flatter, with less forest but wide expanses of heath, moorland and scrub, and several large tracts of peat moss, desolate and impossible to cultivate, though the locals who knew the safe dykes cut and stacked fuel there for their winter use'. Since the beginning of the eighteenth century much of this 'wilderness of dark-brown pools and quaking mosses and tangled bush' has been reclaimed by drainage.

In the vicinity of the small market town of Ellesmere there are a number of lakes or meres which were formed by glacial activity some 20,000 years ago, during the last Ice Age. The Mere, the largest of the lakes in the Shropshire and Cheshire plain, lies to the east of Ellesmere and contains two artificial islands which are frequented by numerous species of sea and freshwater birds, including herons, grebes, gulls and a variety of ducks.

'Ellesmere, with its meres and peat mosses, lies on the watershed of the rivers Dee and Severn, and the basins of these two great water-ways exhibit very distinct contours and vegetation,' says Harold Peake, in his *Historical Guide to Ellesmere*, published in 1897. He goes on to describe the differences between the landscapes of the Severn and the Dee, concluding with a description of the

*The village of Montford lies on the north bank of the River Severn, some four miles north-west of Shrewsbury and one mile south-west of Montford Bridge. The red sandstone Church of St Chad, standing proudly on the top of the hill, serves both villages. Dating from the thirteenth century, it was rebuilt in 1737–38 by William Cooper of Shrewsbury and restored in 1884. The parents of Charles Darwin, who was born at Shrewsbury in 1809, are buried in the churchyard. The village of Montford Bridge grew up around the bridge which carries the main road from Shrewsbury to Oswestry over the River Severn. There has been a bridge at Montford since ancient times, when it was chosen by Welsh princes and English earls as a place for parley.*

*Shrawardine Castle*

*Just over one mile to the west of Montford is the hamlet of Shrawardine where there are the remains of a Norman castle, probably built by Reginald the Sheriff at the end of the eleventh century. After being destroyed by the Welsh in 1215 the castle was rebuilt by John FitzAlan. Shrawardine castle was captured by the Parliamentarians in June 1645, after a five-day siege, and then destroyed. All that remain today are a few standing fragments thought to belong to the medieval keep*

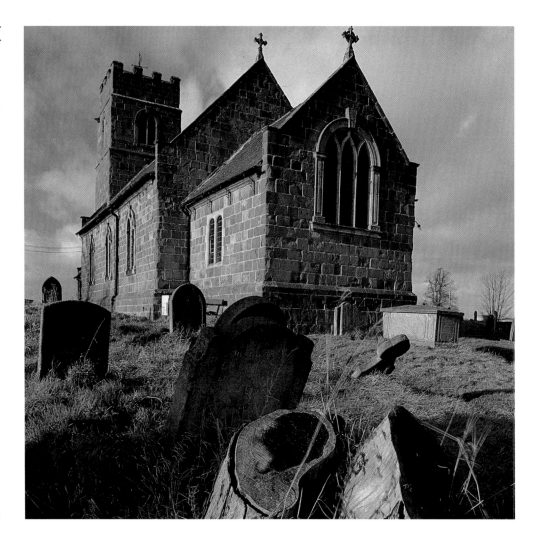

*Church of St Chad, Montford*

*Haughmond Abbey: looking across the remains of the Abbot's private chamber towards the infirmary hall*

*Prees Heath, near Whitchurch*

*The extensive ruins of Haughmond Abbey are situated some three miles north-east of Shrewsbury and beneath the wooded slopes of Haughmond Hill. The abbey was founded by William FitzAlan in about 1135 for a community of Augustinian canons and was considerably rebuilt as they prospered. After its dissolution in 1539, the church and many of the monastic buildings were demolished. Most of those that survived, which included the Abbot's lodging, the great hall and the kitchens, were incorporated into a private house. It was burnt down during the Civil War. Apart from the doorway leading to the western range of the cloister, all that remain of the twelfth-century abbey church are the foundations. The chapter house, with its three magnificent carved arches, also dates from the twelfth century.*

*Countryside near the Manor of*
*Lai (Lowe)*

'In the twilight of the softer, more open country in the north-east of the shire, where day lingered longer than among the folded hills of the western border, Nicholas Harnage rode between flat, rich fields, unwontedly dried by the heat, into the wattled enclosure of the manor of Lai. Wrapped round on all sides by the enlarged fields of the plain, sparsely tree'd to make way for wide cultivation, the house rose long and low, a stone-built hall and chambers over a broad undercroft, with stables and barns about the interior of the fence. Fat country, good for grain and for roots, with ample grazing for any amount of cattle. The byres were vocal as Nicholas entered at the gate, the mild, contented lowing of well-fed beasts, milked and drowsy.'

*An Excellent Mystery*

plants and vegetation found in and around the meres. 'But perhaps,' he adds, 'the greatest interest centres in the peat mosses. Here one may walk for yards, and woe betide the person who stands still, supported on what turns out to be nothing more than a continuous bed of floating *sphagnum*. Doubtless such a journey is attended with some danger; but what of that? The risk only adds a zest to the enterprise, and the botanist treasures the more highly the prizes he has gained in this way.'

In the *Eighth Chronicle* Peter Clemence, the envoy of Bishop Henry of Blois, was feared lost in the treacherous peat-hags near Whitchurch, 'twenty miles and more north' of Shrewsbury. When Hugh Beringar journeyed north to search for the missing man, and found only his horse, he was warned that the 'mosses were no place for a stranger to go by night, and none too safe for a rash traveller even by day. The peat-pools, far down, held bones enough.'

In marked contrast to the flat landscape of the Shropshire plain, the land to the south-west of the Severn is mainly uplands, varying from wild and barren heathland to forested hills, and from wind-swept rocky summits to sheltered and fertile valleys. The underlying rock, too, is varied, ranging from the ancient molten lavas and volcanic ashes that form the Wrekin, Caer Caradoc Hill, The Lawley and Earl's Hill near Pontesbury, to name but a few, to the pale limestones of the Wenlock Edge escarpment and the warm sandstones of the Long Mynd plateau.

Twelve miles south-west of Shrewsbury are the Stiperstones, a jagged ridge of hard white quartzite, which was shattered into regular block-like patterns by frost action during the last Ice Age. At 1,762 feet above sea-level they are the second highest of the Shropshire hills and were bought in 1981 by the Nature Conservancy Council, who have designated the area a National Nature Reserve. Apart from the dramatic rubble-strewn outcrops of the Stiperstones, most of the 1,015-acre reserve is heathland, covered with heather, gorse and bilberries (known locally as wimberries), and is the habitat of many moorland birds, including pipits, curlews and red grouse.

The Long Mountain and the remote hills around Clun Forest and the Ludlow area are formed mainly of sandstone. Included among these are the Clee Hills, situated in the extreme south of the county, which are capped with a layer of hard volcanic rock called dolerite, known locally as dhustone (Dhustone is also the name of a small hamlet situated a short distance south of Titterstone Clee). These hills, the highest of which is Brown Clee Hill, almost 1,800 feet above sea-level, are featured in the *Sixth Chronicle (The Virgin in the Ice)* and contained the hidden stronghold of the outlaw Alain le Gaucher and his murderous band of followers (see Ludlow and the South, p. 137).

*Moreton Corbet Castle*

*Eight miles north-east of Shrewsbury and to the west of the River Roden is the village of Moreton Corbet and the ruins of a medieval castle. The shell of a stately mansion, started in the late sixteenth century and never completed, overshadows the remains of the Norman fortress. The building, incorporating parts of the castle, was begun by Robert Corbet who, it is said, was inspired to build the mansion after returning from a trip to Italy. A Royalist stronghold, the house and castle were besieged by the Parliamentarians during the Civil War and both were extensively damaged*

*Caer Caradoc Hill and the Lawley*

ABOVE *and* BELOW: *Pontesford Hill*

Caer Caradoc Hill and the Lawley were formed by volcanic lava and ash some 900 million years ago and are part of the miniature mountain range of the Stretton Hills which lie between the Long Mynd and the steep limestone escarpment of Wenlock Edge. Caer Caradoc, at 1,506 feet, is the highest of the Stretton Hills. On its summit are the earthwork remains of an Iron Age hill-fort and from here, it is said, Caradoc made a heroic stand against the Roman army.

The village of Pontesbury is dominated by the volcanic outcrop of Pontesford Hill, its two summits each crowned with the earthwork remains of an Iron Age hill-fort. The southernmost summit, known as Earl's Hill, reaches a height of 1,050 feet, and is now a nature reserve cared for by the Shropshire Trust for Nature Conservation. The hill and those nearby have been mined for lead for centuries and some of the old workings date back to Roman times.

The Long Mynd is a six-mile-long range of rounded hills, with a broad and undulating moorland plateau rising to nearly 1,700 feet at Pole Bank. It lies to the west of All Stretton, Church Stretton and Little Stretton. Much of the Long Mynd is owned by the National Trust; farmers in the surrounding villages have the right to graze their sheep and ponies on the common land.

*Carding Mill Valley, the Long Mynd*

*Looking east towards the Stretton Hills from Haddon Hill on the Long Mynd*

*The Stiperstones looking towards the Welsh Hills*

The Stiperstones are reputed to have been the haunt of Shropshire witches and there is a legend that the Devil himself used to attend, presiding over their gatherings from the Devil's Chair, the highest of the rugged peaks along the ridge. There are two traditions surrounding the formation of the Devil's Chair. The first is that the Devil constructed the chair in the hope that his weight would cause England to sink beneath the sea. The second is that the Devil was carrying a pile of boulders in his apron when the string broke and they were scattered along the ridge, hence the broken, rubble-strewn appearance of the landscape. Edric the Wild is also reputed to have been imprisoned underground in the nearby lead mines and can sometimes be heard trying to dig his way out. On occasions, however, he is said to have broken free to haunt the nearby hills in the shape of a large black dog with fiery eyes. It is further alleged that if Edric is seen riding with his followers along the Stiperstones it heralds the outbreak of war.

'There were other lords of manors who allowed certain days for the gathering of wild fruits or dead wood, but in the nearby reaches of the Long Forest the lazar-house [of Saint Giles] had the right to make forays for wood, both for fuel and fencing or other building uses, on four days in the year, one in October, one in November, one in December, whenever the weather allowed, and one in February or March to replenish stocks run down by the winter.'

The Devil's Novice

*The Long Forest south of Brace Meole (Meole Brace)*

During the period of the *Chronicles* most of Shropshire, but particularly the region south of Shrewsbury and the Severn, was covered in forest. The great belt of woodland that stretched westward from Beistan (Bayston Hill) almost into Wales was known as the Long Forest and is vividly described in the *Tenth Chronicle (The Pilgrim of Hate)*:

> In the parcel of old forest north and west of the hamlet of Hanwood there were groves where stray outlaws could find ample cover, provided they stayed clear of the few settlements within reach. Local people tended to fence their holdings and band together to protect their own small ground. The forest was for plundering, poaching, pasturing of swine, all with secure precautions. Travellers, though they might call on hospitality and aid where needed, must fend for themselves in the thicker coverts, if they cared to venture through them. By and large, safety here in Shropshire under Hugh Beringar was as good as anywhere in England.

The landscape of Shropshire is rich and varied, with heather-clad hills, wild windswept heights, reed-filled marshland, treacherous peat bogs, spectacular gorges, hidden valleys, lush and fertile plains, desolate moorland, dense forests, luxuriant water-meadows, nutrient-rich lakes, cultivated fields, salmon- and trout-frequented rivers and streams, barren mountains of spoil from abandoned quarries and mines, ancient woodland and deer-stocked parks. Almost in the heart and centre of this land of contrasts is the county town of Shrewsbury, where Cadfael, the 'Welshman from Gwynedd, by way of Antioch and Jerusalem, and only God knew where else', came in his middle years to enter the Benedictine house of Saint Peter and Saint Paul. Yet, as he once sadly admitted to his friend Hugh Beringar, he was not sure that he could support the monastic life without those 'stolen excursions' outside the abbey walls. And, more often than not, those excursions took him away from Shrewsbury and into the surrounding countryside of Shropshire; a land bordering on his native Wales and treasured above all others, in which of his own free will he chose to spend the rest of his long and active life.

*The uplands of the Long Forest*

 *'This was not yet border country, but close kin to it, heaving into fretful outcrops that broke the thin soil, bearing heather and coarse upland grasses, scrub bushes and sparsity trees, then bringing forth prodigal life roofed by very old trees in every wet hollow. A little further on this course, and the close, dark woods began, tall top cover, heavy interweaving of middle growth, and a tangle of bush and bramble and ground-cover below. Undisturbed forest, though here and there were rare islands of tillage bright and open within it, every one an astonishment.'*

*The Pilgrim of Hate*

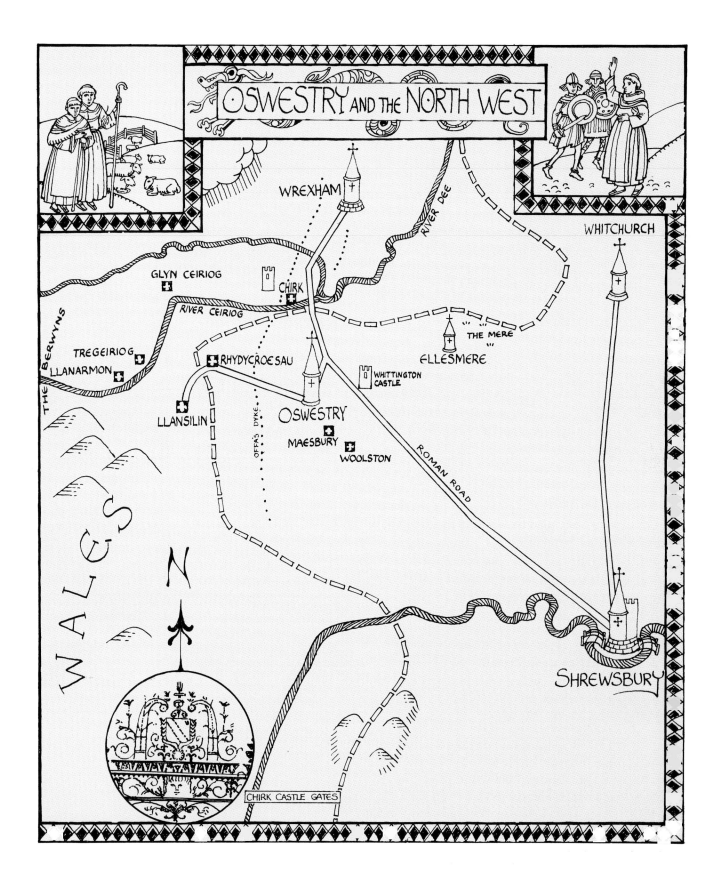

OSWESTRY AND THE NORTH WEST

WREXHAM

RIVER DEE

WHITCHURCH

GLYN CEIRIOG

CHIRK

RIVER CEIRIOG

THE BERWYNS

TREGEIRIOG

LLANARMON

RHYDYCROESAU

THE MERE

ELLESMERE

WHITTINGTON CASTLE

LLANSILIN

OFFA'S DYKE

OSWESTRY

MAESBURY

WOOLSTON

ROMAN ROAD

WALES

N

SHREWSBURY

CHIRK CASTLE GATES

# Oswestry and the North-West

hrunken like a bird, and toothless', old Brother Rhys spent most of his time confined to the infirmary of Shrewsbury Abbey and was 'considered mildly senile, his wanderings timeless and disorganised'. He was born, in his own words, '"nearby the church of Llansilin, which is the centre of the commote of Cynllaith. Welsh land from the beginning of the world!"' Llansilin is a small village about five miles due west of Oswestry, on the Welsh side of the border.

In December of the year 1138, according to the *Third Chronicle of Brother Cadfael (Monk's-Hood)*, Brother Cadfael, who had business in the north-west of the shire, agreed to carry greetings from Brother Rhys to his kinfolk on the borderland. Shrewsbury Abbey owned land in the remote hills of Rhydycroesau nearby, where two of the Benedictine brothers looked after a flock of about two hundred sheep. When one of the brothers took sick, word was sent to the abbey, and Cadfael was promptly dispatched to doctor the ailing man.

The road from Shrewsbury to Oswestry was one of the main highroads of the region, and fairly well maintained. The old people, the Romans, had laid it long ago when they ruled in Britain, and the same road ran south-eastward right to the city of London, where King Stephen was now preparing to keep Christmas among his lords, and Cardinal-bishop Alberic of Ostia was busy holding his legatine council for the reform of the church, to the probable discomfiture of Abbot Heribert. But here, riding in the opposite direction, the road ran straight and wide, only a little over-grown with grass here and there, and encroached upon by the wild verges, through fat farming country and woods to the town of Oswestry, a distance of no more than eighteen miles. Cadfael took it at a brisk but steady pace, to keep the mule content.

*Some five miles west of Oswestry and twenty miles north-west of Shrewsbury, Llansilin is a small village lying on rising ground above the valley of the River Cynllaith. The Church of St Silin, from which the village takes its name, dates from the thirteenth century, but was later remodelled; during the nineteenth century it was heavily restored. The damage to the door of the church, which is pockmarked with holes, is reputed to have been caused by bullets fired during the Civil War. The enormous yew trees in the churchyard are of great antiquity and would certainly have been standing when Shrewsbury Abbey was founded in 1083.*

*Church of St Silin, Llansilin, Clwyd*

*Rhydycroesau*

'*Cadfael discerned a deep tranquil satisfaction in the shepherd's life. The children of his solicitude were seldom killed, unless disease, injury or decrepitude threatened, or in time of desperation the flock could not all be fed through the winter. Their wool and milk were of more value than their meat, and their precious skins could be garnered only once, and better when for distress they had to be slaughtered. So they remained through their natural lives, growing into familiarity and affection, trusting and being understood, even acquiring names. Shepherds had a community of their own, people with gentle, obstinate, quiet companions, who did no murder or theft or banditry, broke no laws, made no complaints, fuelled no rebellions.*

'*All the same, he thought, climbing the hill in long, easy strides, I could not be a shepherd for long. I should miss all the things I deplore, the range and grasp of man for good and evil. And instantly he was back with the struggles and victories and victims of the day.*'

*Monk's-Hood*

Beyond the town it was but four miles to the sheepfolds. In the distance, as he rode due west in the dimming light, the hills of Wales rose blue and noble, the great rolling ridge of Berwyn melting into a faintly misted sky.

He came to the small, bare grange in a fold of the hills before dark. A low, solid wooden hut housed the brothers, and beyond lay the much larger byres and stables, where the sheep could be brought in from ice and snow, and beyond again, climbing the gentle slopes, the long, complex grey-stone walls of the field enclosures, where they grazed in this relatively mild beginning of winter, and were fed roots and grain if ever stubble and grass failed them. The hardiest were still out at liberty in the hills.

It was not the first time, nor was it the last, that Cadfael had travelled to Oswestry and crossed the 'old boundary dyke' into Wales. In the *First Chronicle (A Morbid Taste for Bones)* he had joined Prior Robert's expedition to acquire the bones of Saint Winifred from the remote Welsh village of Gwytherin (see Saint Winifred, p. 85). The journey had taken the monks through the north-west of the shire; on their return, the reliquary containing the holy relics of the saint was, reputedly, put down near Woolston, where a miraculous well appeared (now known as Saint Winifred's Well). Hugh Beringar, according to the *Chronicles*, owned a manor at Maesbury, a small village just over a mile north-west of the well, and three miles due south of Oswestry.

In the *Ninth Chronicle (Dead Man's Ransom)* Cadfael once again journeyed to Oswestry and the north-west. The *Chronicle* opens after the defeat of King Stephen at the Battle of Lincoln in February 1141. Gilbert Prestcote, Sheriff of Shropshire, is badly injured in the fighting and is taken prisoner by the Welsh under Cadwaladr of Gwynedd and Madog ap Meredith of Powys. At the same time, Earl Ranulf of Chester, encouraged by his victory at Lincoln, threatens to disrupt the peace, not only along the Cheshire and Shropshire border but also along the English border with Wales. However, the brother of Cadwaladr, Prince Owain Gwynedd, 'Lord of North Wales', who had 'never put his hand in the fire for the Empress', comes 'east out of his eyrie to keep a weather eye upon Ranulf of Chester, who might be so blown up with his success as to mistake the mettle of the Prince of Gwynedd'.

It is in this hostile and lawless climate that Hugh Beringar, Gilbert's deputy, asks Brother Cadfael if he would make the journey north to try and contact Owain. His mission is twofold: to attempt to locate the whereabouts of the injured sheriff and, if he is found to be in Wales, to investigate the possibility of exchanging him for a Welsh prisoner recently captured during a skirmish in the Long Forest, south-west of Shrewsbury.

'I have a border to keep and a garrison to conserve,' said Hugh, 'and neighbours across the border drunk on their own prowess, all too likely to be running wild in search of more conquests. Getting word through to Owain Gwynedd is a risky

*Offa's Dyke, near
Carreg-y-Big*

*In the latter half of the eighth century Offa, King of Mercia, ordered the
construction of a huge earthwork mound and ditch to mark the boundary between
England and Wales. It stretched, with some gaps, from the Bristol Channel near
Chepstow in the south to the Irish Sea near Prestatyn in the north. Although the
distance of the boundary was about 150 miles, Offa's Dyke accounted for only
eighty miles of the total. It consisted of a bank some sixty feet high with a ditch some
twelve feet deep on the Welsh side. After 1,200 years sections of the dyke are still in
evidence. In 1971 Offa's Dyke Path – a long-distance footpath totalling 176 miles
– was opened, following about sixty miles of the best-preserved stretches of the dyke.*

*Standing Stone, near
Rhydycroesau*

*Standing Stone, near
Carreg-y-Big*

John Corbet Anderson, in his Shropshire: its Early History and Antiquities *(1864) mentions that there 'are two hoar stones in the neighbourhood of Oswestry; one six feet ten inches above the surface, and three feet six inches across the western face, lies near Offa's Dyke. It goes by the name of Carreg-y-Big or The Pointed Stone. The other hoar stone, which is called Garreg Lwyd or The Great Hoary Stone, measures nine feet by three, and lies a few yards to the right of the Holyhead road, a mile on the Shrewsbury side of Oswestry.' Anderson goes on to define a hoar stone as 'an ancient, single upright and unhewn stone of memorial, erected to define the limits of territory. The actual hoar stones that now exist are few.' There is another (marked on the Ordnance Survey map as a Standing Stone) three miles west of Oswestry, near the hamlet of Rhydycroesau.*

*The ruins of Whittington Castle are situated on low-lying ground in the village of Whittington, some two miles north-east of Oswestry. It was once surrounded and protected by marshland and, although the land has since been drained, the wide moat still contains water. A castle may have been built by Roger de Montgomery, on the site of the present castle, at the end of the eleventh century. At the beginning of the thirteenth century it belonged to Fulk Fitz Warin, who rebuilt and enlarged the earlier fortress. It was attacked by the Welsh on a number of occasions and in 1223 it was reputedly captured by Llywelyn the Great. The castle was soon retaken, however, and remained the property of the Fitz Warin family until the fifteenth century when it was given by Henry VI to the Earl of Stafford. By the middle of the following century the castle was in a bad state of repair and it subsequently fell into ruin. In about 1760 much of the stone was used to repair the road between Whittington and Halston. The outer gateway was repaired with stone from one of the towers in 1809. Near the restored thirteenth-century gatehouse, with its two drum towers and broad archway, is a small timber-framed house.*

business and we all know it. I would be dubious of letting a captain loose on that mission who lacks Welsh, for I might never see hide nor hair of him again. Even a well-armed party of five or six could vanish. You're Welsh, and have your habit for a coat of mail, and once across the border you have kin everywhere. I reckon you a far better hazard than any battle party. With a small escort, in case of masterless men, and your Welsh tongue and net of kindred to tackle any regular company that crosses you. What do you say?'

'I should be ashamed, as a Welshman,' said Cadfael comfortably, 'if I could not recite my pedigree back sixteen degrees, and some of my kin are here across the border of this shire, a fair enough start towards Gwynedd.'

'Ah, but there's word that Owain may not be so far distant as the wilds of Gwynedd. With Ranulf of Chester so set up in his gains, and greedy for more, the Prince has come east to keep an eye on his own. So the rumours say. There's even a whisper he may be on our side of the Berwyns, in Cynllaith or Glyn Ceiriog, keeping a close watch on Chester and Wrexham.'

Cadfael, with 'his knot of light-armed men about him', left Shrewsbury by 'the Welsh bridge, and made good speed over the near reaches of their way, north-west towards Oswestry'.

Oswestry is a border market town, nestling in the foothills of Wales. It lies in the north-west corner of Shropshire and, being a frontier post, has been ruled by both the Welsh and the English at different stages of its history. The Domesday Book does not mention Oswestry, but it does refer to a castle built by Rainald, Sheriff of Shropshire, in the Merset hundred, near Meresberie (Maesbury). All

*Whittington Castle*

*Parish Church of St Oswald, Oswestry*

*The large parish church of St Oswald dates from Norman times. After being damaged during the Civil War, it was substantially rebuilt in 1675, and in 1872–74 it was restored by G. E. Street. Further restorations took place in 1955 and 1977*

*Old Oswestry hill-fort*

*Old Oswestry Iron Age hill-fort, covering forty acres, was abandoned after the Roman Conquest and, except for a brief period during the Dark Ages and perhaps in the Middle Ages, remained unoccupied*

that now remains of this Norman fortress stands in a small park in the centre of Oswestry, near Horsemarket. To the north of the town, however, are the extensive earthworks of an Iron Age hill-fort, dating back to at least the fifth century BC. Oswestry was named after Saint Oswald, the Christian King of Northumbria, who was slain at the Battle of Maserfelth or Maserfield (believed to be Oswestry) in 642 by the pagan King Penda of Mercia.

In 1141, when Cadfael journeyed north to find the Welsh Prince Owain Gwynedd, Oswestry Castle was held by the Normans for King Stephen. Eight years later it was captured by the Welsh under Madog ap Meredith of Powys, who rebuilt it and ruled over the lordship of Oswestry until 1157.

From Oswestry Cadfael and his party turned west, crossed the eighth-century earthwork-barrier of Offa's Dyke and headed for the *maenol* of Tudur ap Rhys at Tregeiriog.

*St Oswald's Well, Oswestry*

*The town of Oswestry was a Saxon settlement and took its name from St Oswald, who was killed at the battle of Maserfield in 642. Legend says that an eagle picked up one of St Oswald's dismembered arms, flew into the air with it and then dropped it. At the spot where it landed a miraculous spring of water bubbled out of the ground, hence the origination of St Oswald's Well at Maserfield, Oswestry*

> Cadwaladr might have had his frolics on his way back to his castle at Aberystwyth with his booty and his prisoners, but to the north of his passage Owain Gwynedd had kept a fist clamped down hard upon disorder. Cadfael and his escort had had one or two brushes with trouble, after leaving Oswestry on their right and plunging into Wales, but on the first occasion the three masterless men who had put an arrow across their path thought better of it when they saw what numbers they had challenged, and took themselves off at speed into the brush; and on the second, an unruly patrol of excitable Welsh warmed into affability at Cadfael's unruffled Welsh greeting, and ended giving them news of the prince's movements. Cadfael's numerous kinsfolk, first and second cousins and shared forbears were warranty enough over much of Clwyd and part of Gwynedd.

Brother Cadfael duly delivered Hugh Beringar's message to Owain Gwynedd at Tregeiriog, who welcomed 'any motion of amity' from Shropshire, where he 'could do with an assured peace'.

> Cadfael had seen him once before, a few years past, and he was not a man to be easily forgotten, for all he made very little ado about state and ceremony, barring the obvious royalty he bore about his own person. He was barely thirty-seven years old, in his vigorous prime; very tall for a Welshman, and fair, after his grandmother Ragnhild of the Danish kingdom of Dublin, and his mother Angharad, known for her flaxen hair among the dark women of the south.

Although the injured Gilbert Prestcote was eventually located and exchanged for the Welsh hostage, he was murdered in the infirmary of Shrewsbury Abbey and Hugh Beringar, as his deputy, assumed the office of Sheriff. The outcome of Cadfael's and Hugh's meeting with Owain Gwynedd is a peaceful alliance, brought about by the discovery that both Owain and Hugh, in the new Sheriff's words, '"have a common interest in the north of this shire, and a common

*Offa's Dyke, near Craignant*

enemy trying his luck there. Wales is in no danger from me and my shire, I believe, in no danger from Wales. At least," Hugh added, reconsidering briskly, "not from Gwynedd."'

The danger, it seemed, was no longer from the Welsh of Gwynedd, nor immediately from Ranulf of Chester, but further south, along the border near Welshpool, from Madog ap Meredith and the Welsh of Powys (see The Welsh Border, p. 131).

*Set in parkland just over a mile west of Chirk and five miles north of Oswestry, Chirk Castle is a unique example of a Marcher, or border, fortress. Built on the site of an earlier castle, it was started in the reign of Edward I by the powerful Marcher lord, Roger Mortimer, and completed by 1310. Although there has been much rebuilding over the centuries, the exterior form of the walls and towers has survived almost unchanged since the beginning of the fourteenth century, apart from the insertion of windows. Authorities differ as to the reason for the truncated towers: some maintain that they were never completed, while others claim that they were reduced in height after the Civil War. The approach to the castle is through a pair of magnificent wrought-iron gates, fashioned in 1721 by the Davies brothers of Bersham, near Wrexham. The castle is in the care of the National Trust.*

*Chirk Castle, Clwyd*

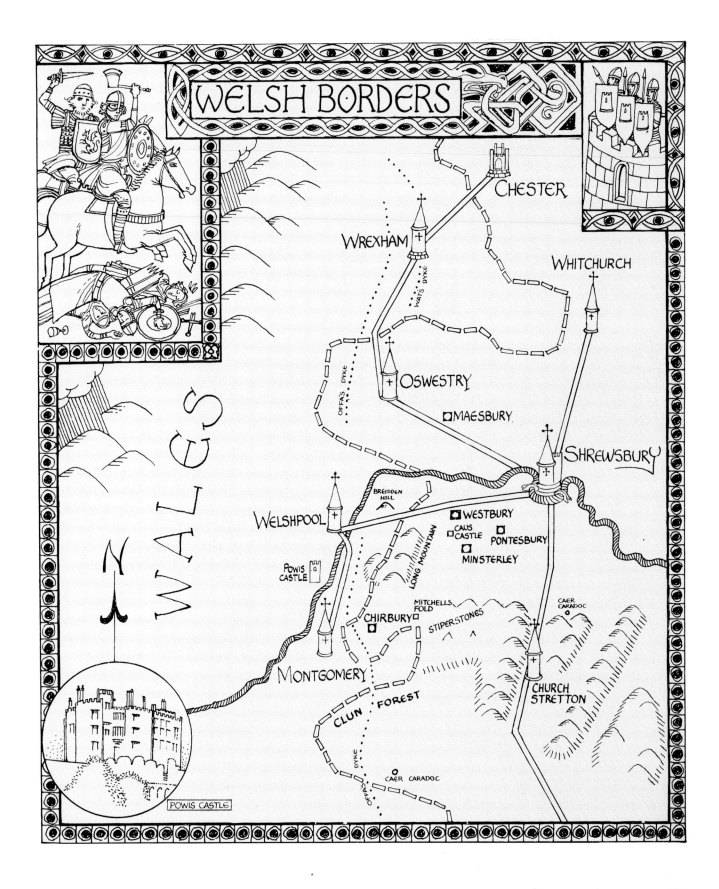

WELSH BORDERS

CHESTER

WREXHAM

WHITCHURCH

OSWESTRY

WATS DYKE

OFFA'S DYKE

MAESBURY

SHREWSBURY

WELSHPOOL

BREIDDEN HILL

WESTBURY

CAUS CASTLE

PONTESBURY

MINSTERLEY

POWIS CASTLE

LONG MOUNTAIN

MITCHELLS FOLD

STIPERSTONES

CAER CARADOC

CHIRBURY

WALES

N

MONTGOMERY

CLUN FOREST

OFFA'S DYKE

CAER CARADOC

CHURCH STRETTON

POWIS CASTLE

# The Welsh Border

uring prehistoric times successive waves of immigrants, coming from different parts of Europe, arrived in Britain and either merged with the native population or drove the earlier inhabitants west to seek refuge in the mountains of Wales or the western part of England. Among these immigrants were the people of the Bronze Age, a short and thick-set race with black hair who came from the western Mediterranean in about 1700 BC, and the people of the Iron Age, a tall and fair-complexioned race, known as Celts, who came from Central Europe in about 500 BC. Both races have left evidence of their existence in Shropshire: examples of the burial mounds of the former can be found in hilly areas like the Long Mynd, while their stone circles can be found at Mitchell's Fold, on Stapeley Hill, and at the Hoarstone Circle, near Black Marsh; remains of the hill-forts of the latter, of which the county has twenty-five or so, can be found not only along the western border but also on isolated hills like the Wrekin.

It is thought that when the Romans invaded Britain in the first century AD, much of Shropshire was governed from the Iron Age fort on the Wrekin, which is estimated to have had a population of nearly a thousand. At the time there were three tribes inhabiting the area of present-day Shropshire and the regions adjacent to it: the Cornovii (the tribe whose administrative centre was on the Wrekin), who controlled the area east of the Severn towards Staffordshire and extending northwards to the Mersey; the Ordovices, whose territory extended from the western side of the Severn into central Wales; and the Silures, whose country extended from South Wales and the Bristol Channel into the southern part of the county. The Silures, who were the most savage and warlike of the British tribes, held out longest against the Romans.

*Mitchell's Fold, Stapeley Hill*

*Mitchell's Fold on Stapeley Hill, two miles east of Chirbury, was erected by the people of the Bronze Age over 3,500 years ago, probably for religious purposes. Only fifteen stones remain out of what is thought to have originally been thirty-seven. The ring, about eighty feet in diameter, does not form a true circle. There are a number of legends associated with the stones. It is reputed, for example, that one of the stones, probably the largest, is an old witch called Mitchell, who was turned into stone by a fairy after she had milked the magical cow of Stapeley Hill dry. The cow had been sent to the hill by the fairy, to provide the local inhabitants with an everlasting supply of milk on condition that they came with only one vessel. The witch had tricked the cow into yielding all its milk by using a sieve. The other stones in the circle were erected in order to stop her from escaping.*

As the conquering legions pushed farther westwards, the various tribes they encountered, including the Cornovii, were soon subjugated. Those who refused to accept Roman rule fled west, across the flat plain of the Severn valley and into the wild, inhospitable hills of Wales. By AD 48 the Romans had secured an important strategic base in the area around Wroxeter from which to launch campaigns westwards into the Welsh mountains, which had become the last stronghold of Celtic-British resistance.

The leader of the Iron Age Silures was Caradoc, or Caratacus, the son of Cymbeline or Cunobelinus, King of the British tribe of Catuvellauni. Although he came from another tribe, Caradoc's superior military training, combined with the fierce, warlike nature of the Silures, made them formidable opponents to the Romans. For several years Caradoc stubbornly resisted their attempts to conquer the western tribes, setting up fortified camps on the hills along the border. The remains of one such hill-fort can be found on Caer Caradoc Hill, north-east of Church Stretton in Shropshire, which is named after the chieftain himself. Opposition was so strong that even after Caradoc's defeat and capture in AD 51, it took the Romans almost another thirty years to complete their conquest of Wales.

*Clun Castle*

*The building of Clun Castle is attributed to Picot de Say at the end of the eleventh century. In about 1150, it became the property of the FitzAlans who held the castle until the middle of the sixteenth century when it passed by marriage to the Howards, Dukes of Norfolk. During the reign of Elizabeth I, when it is thought to have been in a totally ruinous state, the castle became the property of the Crown. It was regained by the Dukes of Norfolk in 1603, sold in 1677 and repurchased by the Howards in about 1896. The remains of the Norman border fortress stand on the hillside above the town, overlooking the valley of the River Clun*

After the Roman withdrawal in about AD 410, Wales – left without a military presence to enforce law and order – became a country divided, with various princes and petty chieftains fighting one another for territory. During this turbulent period, with the Britons intent on attacking each other, the defence of the island was ignored and, in consequence, the inhabitants found themselves unable to halt a fresh invasion of migrating peoples from Europe.

These new arrivals came from northern Germany and Scandinavia and included a variety of races (Angles, Saxons and Jutes) who, collectively, became known as the Anglo-Saxons, and, eventually, the English. Once again, the native inhabitants of Britain either fled west or were absorbed by the conquering peoples. After the native Britons had been subdued, however, or driven westwards into Cumbria, Wales and Cornwall, the Anglo-Saxon kingdoms began to war among themselves.

In the seventh century the area now called Shropshire was part of the kingdom of Mercia and was under the rule of a king named Penda, who had killed Oswald, King of Northumbria, at the Battle of Maserfelth in 642. Penda himself was slain at Winwaed, near Leeds, in another battle against the Northumbrians in 655. Further battles took place throughout England, including the Shropshire Battle of Pontesbury in 661. It was by about this time that the surviving Britons had become 'Welsh', or 'foreigners', and their land a distinct country into which the Anglo-Saxons, with a few initial exceptions, were unable to penetrate in force further west than Oswestry.

By the end of the eighth century, when King Offa raised a massive earthwork dyke along the western boundary of his Mercian kingdom, the Celtic-Britons living beyond it, in Wales, described themselves as the *Cymry*, the fellow-countrymen. These Welshmen had their own language and laws and, as the *Chronicles of Brother Cadfael* say, 'preferred their own ancient Celtic Christianity, the solitary hermitage of the self-exiled saint and the homely little college of Celtic monks rather than the shrewd and vigorous foundations that looked to Rome'.

Wales itself was divided into numerous independent warring territories (ruled by self-proclaimed princes and kings), which included Powys and Gwynedd, both mentioned in the *Chronicles*. Yet, as the *Chronicles* point out, 'all Welsh are kin, even if they slit one another's throats now and then, and manure their sparse and stony fields with fratricidal dead in tribal wars'.

Hywel ap Cadell, or Hywel Dda, who ruled from about 910, claimed to be King of all Wales and, according to tradition, compiled the laws of Wales, known as 'the code of Hywel Dda'. This code governed Wales until about the middle of the sixteenth century, when it was superseded by English law.

Throughout the *Chronicles* there are a number of references to the differences between English and Welsh law. In the *Ninth Chronicle (Dead Man's Ransom)*, for example, Brother Cadfael points out to his friend, Hugh Beringar, Sheriff of Shropshire:

> 'Pardon me, Hugh! I am Welsh and you are English. We Welsh recognise degrees. Theft, theft absolute, without excuse, is our most mortal offence, and therefore we hedge it about with degrees, things which are not theft absolute – taking openly by force, taking in ignorance, taking without leave, providing the offender owns to it, and taking to stay alive, where a beggar has starved three days – no man hangs in Wales for these. Even in dying, even in killing, we acknowledge degrees. We make a distinction between homicide and murder, and even the worst may sometimes be compounded for a lesser price than hanging.'

When a fugitive fled into Wales to escape from English law he became an *alltud*, or outlander, a foreigner deprived of the means to make a living.

> In a country where every native-born man had and knew his assured place in a clan kinship, and the basis of all relationships was establishment on the land, whether as free lord or villein partner in a village community, the man from outside, owning no land here, fitting into no place, was deprived of the very basis of living. His only means of establishing himself was by getting some overlord to make compact with him, give him house-room and a stake in the land, and employ him for whatever skills he could offer. For three generations this bargain between them was revocable at any time, and the outlander might leave at the fair price of dividing his chattels equally with the lord who had given him the means of acquiring them.

When Hywel Dda died in 950 the precarious unity, formerly established by his grandfather, Rhodri Mawr or Rhodri the Great, collapsed. Once again the land was thrown into turmoil, with the Welsh not only fighting the Anglo-Saxons and the marauding Danes but also themselves. It is estimated that in the period between Hywel's death and the Norman Conquest in 1066, thirty-five Welsh rulers were killed by Anglo-Saxons, Danes or fellow-Welshmen.

*Montgomery Castle, Powys*

*The small market town of Montgomery was named after Earl Roger de Montgomery, who built a castle sometime between 1070 and 1074 at Hen Domen, one mile north-west of the present town. His eldest son, Robert de Bellême, acquired the castle after his brother's death. In 1102, because of treason, Henry I banished Robert to Normandy and confiscated his estates. Montgomery Castle was granted to Baldwin de Bollers, whose family owned it until 1214–15 when it was sold to Thomas de Erdington. In 1216, however, King John gave it to Gwenwynwyn, Prince of Powys, and almost immediately it was captured by Llywelyn the Great. Henry III built a second castle (now demolished) at Montgomery in 1223 and three years later the town was granted a royal charter.*

*The Welsh borderland*

 *'There was a merchant of Shrewsbury who dealt in fleeces all up and down the borders both from Wales and from such fat sheep-country as the Cotswolds, and had done an interesting side-trade in information, for Hugh's benefit, in these contrary times. His active usefulness was naturally confined to this period of high summer when the wool clip was up for sale, and many dealers had restricted their movements in these dangerous times, but he was a determined man, intrepid enough to venture well south down the border, towards territory held by the empress. His suppliers had sold to him for some years, and had sufficient confidence in him to hold their clip until he made contact. He had good trading relations as far afield as Bruges in Flanders, and was not at all averse to a large risk when calculating on a still larger profit. Moreover, he took his own risks, rather than delegating these unchancy journeys to his underlings. Possibly he even relished the challenge, for he was a stubborn and stalwart man.'*

*An Excellent Mystery*

Initially, the Norman invaders were too busy consolidating their gains in England to bother with Wales. But when the conquering barons started to quarrel among themselves for larger rewards and positions of seniority, William the Conqueror gave the lands along the Welsh border to the Marcher Lords, a term meaning 'the lords of the border'. These Norman adventurers were allowed to conquer land in Wales with their own private armies and establish independent lordships over which they had almost regal power and jurisdiction. Hugh de Averanche or 'Hugh the Wolf', William's nephew, was given control of Chester and the northern marches, Roger de Montgomery was awarded Shrewsbury and the middle marches, and William FitzOsbern was granted Hereford and the southern marches.

Although the border extended from the mouth of the Wye at Chepstow to the Dee estuary, it was by no means fixed, advancing and receding according to the success or failure of Welsh resistance. The conquest of Wales by the Normans, however, was largely confined to the lowlands and it was only in the lowlands, at least until the thirteenth century, that they managed to establish their castles, manors and towns.

During the period of the *Chronicles*, with England torn by civil war between King Stephen and the Empress Maud, unrest along the Welsh border was rife. In September 1140, according to the *Eighth Chronicle (The Devil's Novice)*,

> Hugh Beringar, deputy-sheriff of Shropshire, came down from his manor of Maesbury to take charge in Shrewsbury, for his superior, Gilbert Prestcote, had departed to join King Stephen at Westminster for his half-yearly visit at Michaelmas, to render account of his shire and its revenues. Between the two of them they had held the county staunch and well-defended, reasonably free from the disorders that racked most of the country, and the abbey had good cause to be grateful to them, for many of its sister houses along the Welsh marches had been sacked, pillaged, evacuated, turned into fortresses for war, some more than once, and no remedy offered. Worse than the armies of King Stephen on the one hand and his cousin the empress on the other – and in all conscience they were bad enough – the land was crawling with private armies, predators large and small, devouring everything, wherever they were safe from any force of law strong enough to contain them. In Shropshire the law had been strong enough, thus far, and loyal enough to care for its own.

In February of the following year, fired by the fact that King Stephen had been 'taken at Lincoln, and carried off prisoner to Gloucester', Earl Ranulf of Chester and Madog ap Meredith of Powys had their greedy eyes on gains across their respective borders. Although Chester, 'elated by success and greedy for still more lands', was harassing the Welsh border of Gwynedd, both were threatening the borders of Shropshire. In the *Ninth Chronicle* Hugh Beringar formed a peaceful alliance with Owain, Prince of Gwynedd, both having a common enemy in Ranulf of Chester, and between them they managed to stem his advance. The Welsh of Powys, however, were mustering along the border near Welshpool to mount a raid deep into the heart of Shropshire.

The Welsh of Powys had done very well out of their Lincoln venture, undertaken rather for plunder than out of any desire to support the earl of Chester, who was more often enemy than ally. Madog ap Meredith was quite willing to act in conjunction with Chester again, provided there was profit in it for Madog, and the news of Ranulf's probes into the borders of Gwynedd and Shropshire alerted him to pleasurable possibilities. It was some years since the men of Powys had captured and partially burned the castle of Caus, after the death of William Corbett and in the absence of his brother and heir, and they had held on to this advanced outpost ever since, a convenient base for further incursions. With Hugh Beringar gone north, and half the Shrewsbury garrison with him, the time seemed ripe for action.

The first thing that happened was a lightning raid from Caus along the valley towards Minsterley, the burning of an isolated farmstead and the driving off of a few cattle. The raiders drew off as rapidly as they had advanced, when the men of Minsterley mustered against them, and vanished into Caus and through the hills into Wales with their booty. But it was indication enough that they might be expected back and in greater strength, since this first assay had passed off so easily and without loss.

*Looking from Middletown Hill towards Wales*

ABOVE: *the view from Caus Castle;*
LEFT: *Caus Castle*

*Soon after the Norman survey of 1086, Roger Fitz Corbet built a castle high on the eastern foothills of the Long Mountain and named it Caus in honour of his birthplace, Pays de Caux in Normandy. After Fitz Corbet's death his eldest son, William Corbet, inherited the castle. In 1134 it was reputedly captured and burnt by the Welsh. It was of such strategic importance, guarding the route from Montgomery to Shrewsbury, that it continued to play an important role in the defence of the borders for centuries afterwards. Towards the close of the thirteenth century there was even a town in the outer bailey. Caus Castle was finally destroyed in 1645 during the Civil War, and all that now remain are the stone foundations and fragments of the keep*

'*Several of the lesser manors in these border regions had declined by reason of their perilous location, and some were half-deserted, leaving their fields untilled. Until April [of the year 1141] the border castle of Caus had been in Welsh hands, an added threat to peaceful occupation, and there had not yet been time since Hugh's reclamation of the castle for the depleted hamlets to re-establish themselves. Moreover, in this high summer it was no hardship to live wild, and skilful poaching and a little profitable thievery could keep two or three good fellows in meat while they allowed time for their exploits in the south to be forgotten, and made up their minds where best to pass the time until a return home seemed possible*'

*The Pilgrim of Hate*

*Rodney Pillar on Breidden Hill*
*from Pritchard's Hill*

*Breidden Hill, formed mostly of volcanic rock, overlooks the valley of the River Severn six miles north of Welshpool. In contrast to Middletown Hill, its immediate neighbour, the eastern slopes of Breidden Hill are thickly afforested. On the summit, 1,199 feet high, are the earthwork remains of an Iron Age hill-fort and also Rodney's Column, a landmark dedicated to Admiral Lord Rodney, who died in 1792. The north-west face of the hill has been subjected to extensive quarrying.*

The next thrust came two days later. 'Madog ap Meredith had been pleased with his first probe, and brought more men into the field before he launched his attack in force. Down the Rea valley to Minsterley they swarmed, burned and looted, wheeled both ways round Minsterley, and flowed on towards Pontesbury.'.

Hearing that the Welsh of Powys were 'swarming in force along the Minsterley valley' and 'halfway to Shrewsbury', Hugh Beringar, having strengthened his northern border at Oswestry, Ellesmere and Whitchurch, rode south with twenty men and Brother Cadfael. They travelled down the border from Llansilin, passing 'to the east of the Breiddens, and down by Westbury to Minsterley', hoping to cut the raiders off and stop them 'from getting back to their base in Caus'.

'"I tire of having men of Powys in that castle," said Hugh, setting his jaw. "We must have it back and make it habitable, and keep a garrison there."'

While Hugh and his men were moving down the border to cut off the warparty's retreat, the garrison at Shrewsbury was sending reinforcements west, led by Alan Herbard. If both parties moved fast enough, it was hoped they might trap the Welsh of Powys 'between the two prongs and crack them like a nut'. They met in the northern uplands of the Long Forest at Godric's Ford, where 'there was a small grange of Benedictine nuns, a cell of the Abbey of Polesworth', and in the short battle that followed the Welsh of Powys were demoralised and defeated.

> It was done, they were gone, vanishing very rapidly and quietly, leaving only the rustling of bushes behind them on the near side of the brook, to make for some distant place where they could cross unseen and unpursued. On the further side, where the bulk of their numbers fled, the din of their flight subsided gradually into the depths of the neglected coppices, seeking thicker cover into which they could scatter and be lost. Hugh was in no haste, he let them salvage their wounded and hustle them away with them, several among them who might, indeed, be dead. There would be cuts and grazes and wounds enough among the defenders; by all means let the Welsh tend their own and bury their own. But he deployed his men, and a dozen or so of Herbard's party, like beaters after game, to herd the Welshmen back methodically into their own country. He had no wish to start a determined bloodfeud with Madog ap Meredith, provided this lesson was duly learned.

*Middletown Hill*

*In Wales, with its north-eastern extremity in England, Middletown Hill stands to the south-east of the heavily wooded slopes of Breidden Hill. On its 1,194 feet high bracken-strewn summit is an Iron Age fortress, known as Cefn y Castell*

*Looking from Middletown Hill towards Wales*

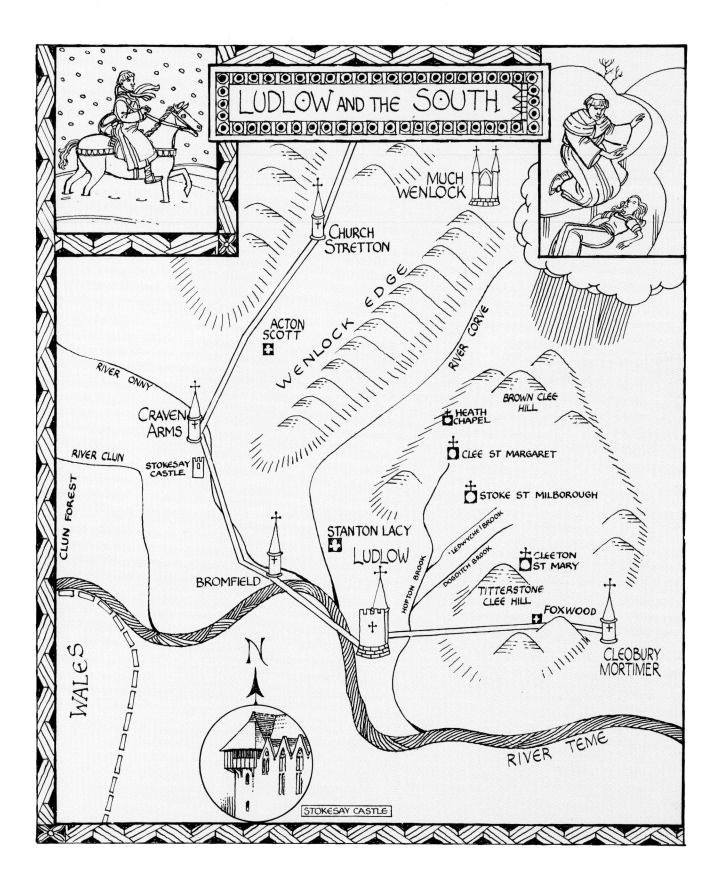

LUDLOW AND THE SOUTH

MUCH WENLOCK

CHURCH STRETTON

WENLOCK EDGE

RIVER CORVE

ACTON SCOTT

RIVER ONNY

BROWN CLEE HILL

HEATH CHAPEL

CRAVEN ARMS

RIVER CLUN

CLEE ST MARGARET

STOKESAY CASTLE

CLUN FOREST

STOKE ST MILBOROUGH

STANTON LACY

LUDLOW

LEDWYCHE BROOK

DOGDITCH BROOK

CLEETON ST MARY

BROMFIELD

HOPTON BROOK

TITTERSTONE CLEE HILL

FOXWOOD

CLEOBURY MORTIMER

WALES

N

RIVER TEME

STOKESAY CASTLE

# Ludlow and the South

The 'first flakes of the first snow of the winter' fell in Shrewsbury on the night of the last day of November 1139. 'The air was full of drifting unease, but the fall was light and fitful here. Further south it set in heavily, borne on a north-westerly wind, dry, fine snow that turned the night into a white, whirling mist, shrouding outlines, burying paths, blown into smooth, breaking waves only to be lifted and hurled again into new shapes. Valleys filled to a treacherous level, hillsides were scoured clean. Wise men stayed within their houses, clapped to shutter and door, and stopped the chinks between the boards, where thin white fingers reached through. The first snow, and the first hard frost.'

Earlier that month the 'tide of civil war, lately so sluggish and inactive', had risen 'suddenly to sweep over the city of Worcester'. Those inhabitants who could get away in time were sent 'scurrying for their lives northwards away from the marauders, to burrow into hiding wherever there was manor or priory, walled town or castle strong enough to afford them shelter'. Some, no doubt, made for the fortified town and castle at Ludlow, situated on the southern border of Shropshire, twenty-seven miles south of Shrewsbury.

Ludlow, surprisingly, is not mentioned in the Domesday survey of 1086. However, it is thought to have been one of the extensive holdings of the Lacy family, whose principal Shropshire manor was at Stanton (now Stanton Lacy), three miles to the north-west of the town. Although some historians credit the foundation of Ludlow Castle to Earl Roger de Montgomery, it is more likely – because of its defensive position close to Stanton – that the founder was Roger de Lacy.

*Judge's Lodgings,*
*Ludlow Castle*

*Ludlow Castle from the valley of*
*the River Teme*

*Situated some twenty-two miles south of Shrewsbury, Ludlow is an attractive market town with a mixture of ancient and modern buildings. It grew up in the shadow of the castle and was designed in the late eleventh century on the grid-iron pattern of most medieval towns. The castle, built of stone from the outset, was erected on a rocky cliff near the confluence of the rivers Teme and Corve, most probably by Roger de Lacy shortly after the Norman Conquest. In the early fourteenth century the property passed by marriage to the powerful Roger Mortimer, first Earl of March. He turned the fortress into a palace. In 1472 it became the administrative centre of the Council for Wales and the Marches, set up by Edward IV to govern the whole of Wales and the border frontier. The Judge's Lodgings were built in 1581 by Sir Henry Sidney to house judges and other important officials when they were in Ludlow attending the courts. After the council was abolished at the end of the seventeenth century the castle was allowed to fall into decay. In 1811 the ruins were purchased from the Crown by the Earl of Powis, who began a programme of preservation and selective repair which continues to this day.*

*The chapel and domestic buildings, Ludlow Castle*

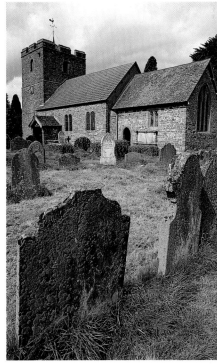

*Church of St John the Baptist, Stokesay*

*About a mile south of the small market town of Craven Arms is Stokesay Castle, dating from the late thirteenth century. At the time of the Domesday Book the manor of Stoke belonged to Roger de Lacy, but by 1115 it had been granted to Theodoric de Say, whose ancestor Picot de Say was Lord of Clun in 1086. Throughout their ownership the family gave parts of Stokesay, including the church, to Haughmond Abbey. The estate passed to John de Vernon in the mid-thirteenth century and in about 1281 the whole manor became the property of Laurence de Ludlow, a wealthy wool merchant, who died in 1296. He built a mansion on the site of an earlier building and, under licence from Edward I, turned it into a fortified manor house. Although it was besieged during the Civil War the royal garrison quickly surrendered and the castle suffered little damage. The approach to the castle is through an attractive timber-framed sixteenth-century gatehouse. Across the moat, the church, with its Norman doorway, was badly damaged during the Civil War. It was largely rebuilt during the Commonwealth at a time when few churches were being built.*

Having helped William of Normandy conquer England in 1066, Walter de Lacy was rewarded with the manor of Stanton. After his death in 1085, his son Roger inherited his estates, and, it is thought, soon afterwards began building Ludlow Castle, one of the few fortresses built in stone from the outset.

In 1095 Roger de Lacy rebelled against King William Rufus and was banished. His lands and properties passed to his brother, Hugh de Lacy, who died without heirs some time before 1121. The castle became the property of the Crown and both Henry I and King Stephen entrusted it to their constables, or castellans.

Josce de Dinan was Castellan of Ludlow Castle in 1139 and, according to the *Sixth Chronicle of Brother Cadfael (The Virgin in the Ice)*, there were rumours that he was thinking of transferring his allegiance from Stephen to the Empress Maud:

> All the border towns were at risk, as well from the precarious loyalties of constables and garrisons as from the enterprise of the enemy. More than one lord in this troubled land had already changed his allegiance, more than one would do so in the future, some, perhaps, for the second or third time. Churchmen, barons and all, they were beginning to look first to their own interests, and place their loyalty where it seemed likely to bring them the greater profit. And it would not be long before some of them came to the conclusion that their interests could be served just as well by flouting both contendants for the crown, and setting up on their own account.

Both Cadfael and Hugh Beringar in Shrewsbury had heard that the Castellan at Ludlow was 'casting his eyes towards the empress'. If he 'had indeed been contemplating defection, and thought better of it, Hugh was content to accept his present steadfastness, but with reservations, and was watching him still. Distrust was only one of the lesser horrors of civil war, but saddening enough. It was well that there could still be absolute trust between tried friends. In these days there was no man living who might not suddenly have acute need of a steady and stout back braced against his own.'

*The River Teme*

About two miles north-west of Ludlow and just over a mile from Stanton Lacy was the modest Benedictine priory of Bromfield, situated on the south bank of the River Onny, near its confluence with the Teme. The *Chronicles* state that in the winter of 1139 Brother Elyas, a Benedictine monk of Pershore, had been charged by his abbot to take a finger-bone of Saint Eadburga to Bromfield, where it was to be installed in a shrine. Having delivered the holy relic safely, Elyas left, through a countryside blanketed in snow, to return to his abbey at Pershore. He did not get very far, as the *Sixth Chronicle* relates:

> On the fifth day of December, about noon, a traveller from the south, who had slept the night at Bromfield priory, some twenty-odd miles away, and had the good fortune to find the highroad, at least, in passable condition, brought an urgent message into Shrewsbury abbey. Prior Leonard of Bromfield had been a monk of

*Church of St Mary, Bromfield*

*Bromfield Gatehouse*

*Just over two miles north-west of Ludlow, the village of Bromfield lies near the confluence of the rivers Onny and Teme. Little is known about the early history of Bromfield Priory. What is certain is that by about 1115 Osbert was 'Prior' of Bromfield, and that in 1155 the priory became dependent on the Benedictine Abbey at Gloucester, and remained so until the Dissolution when the monastic buildings were destroyed. The church became the property of Charles Foxe, of nearby Ludford, who converted it into a house. In 1658 it was restored once more to a place of worship. The unique and memorable plaster ceiling was painted in a naive flamboyant style by Thomas Francis in 1672. All that now remains of the priory is the stone and timbered gatehouse, dating from the fourteenth century, which stands near the church.*

*Snowdrifts east of Bromfield*

'They arose at dawn, Cadfael and Hugh and his men, and went out into a world which had again changed its shape in the night, hillocks levelled and hollows filled in, and a spume of fine snow waving like a languid plume from every crest, in the subsiding winds. They took axes with them, and a litter of leather thongs strung between two poles, and a linen cloth to cover her, and they went in dour silence, none of them with anything to say until words were to the point for the grim work in hand. The fall had stopped at the coming of daylight, as it had now ever since that first night when Yves had set off doggedly to trail his errant sister. Iron frost had begun the next night, and that same night some nocturnal beast had ravished and murdered the girl they went out now to seek, for the ice had taken her to itself very shortly after she had been put into an already congealing stream. Of that Cadfael was certain.

'They found her, after some questing and probing in new snow, swept the fresh fall from the ice, and looked down upon her, a girl in a mirror, a girl spun from glass.'

*The Virgin in the Ice*

*The local people 'know this countryside like their own palms. A stranger would have had to lie up somewhere and wait till he could see his way. In these drifts, and with such a wind blowing, and the snow so dry and fine, paths appear and vanish twice in a day and more. You could walk a mile, and think you knew every landmark, and see nothing you recognised on the way back.'*

The Virgin in the Ice

*Snowfields north of Ludlow*

Shrewsbury until his promotion, and was an old friend of Brother Cadfael's, and familiar with his skills.

'In the night,' the messenger reported, 'some decent fellows of that country brought in a wounded man to the priory, found by the wayside stripped and hacked, and left for dead. And half-dead he is, and his case very bad. If he had lain out all night in the frost he'd have been frozen stiff by morning. And Prior Leonard asked would I bring word here to you, for though they've some knowledge of healing, this case is beyond them, and he said you have experience from the wars, and may be able to save the man. If you could come, and bide until he mends – or until the poor soul's lost! – it would be a great comfort and kindness.'

'If abbot and prior give me leave,' said Cadfael, concerned, 'then most gladly. Footpads preying on the roads so close to Ludlow? What are things come to, there in the south?'

Cadfael's request to go and attend the injured Benedictine monk was treated with sympathy by both Prior Robert and Abbot Radulfus. He filled his scrip with those 'medicines, salves and febrifuges not to be found in every infirmary cupboard' and, donning 'stout boots and a thick travelling cloak', he mounted a horse and set off alone for the priory at Bromfield beyond the southern hills.

Around Shrewsbury the snowfalls had been light and powdery, the pattern of white flakes and black soil constantly changing as the wind blew. But as Cadfael rode south the fields grew whiter, the ditches filled. The branches of trees sagged heavily towards the ground under their load, and by mid-afternoon the leaden sky was sagging no less heavily earthwards, in swags of blue-black cloud. If this went on the wolves would be moving down from the hills and prowling hungrily among the haunts of men. Better to be an urchin under a hedgerow, sleeping the winter away, or a squirrel holed up snugly with his hoarded stores. It had been a good autumn for nuts and acorns.

Riding was pleasure to him, even riding alone and in the bitter cold. The chance seldom came his way now, it was one of the delights he had given up for the quiet of the cloister and the sense of having discovered his true place. In every decision there must be some regrets. He hunched his back solidly against the malice of the wind, and saw the first driven flakes, fine as dust, whirl by him and outpace his horse. He was thinking of the man who waited for him at the end of this journey.

Himself a monk, the messenger had said. Of Bromfield? Surely not. If he had been one of theirs they would have named him. A monk loose and alone about the roads in the mid of night? On what errand? Or in flight from what, before he fell into the mercies of robbers and murderers? Others must have ranged through the same countryside, in flight from the rape of Worcester, and where were they now? Perhaps this cowled wanderer had made his way painfully out of the same holocaust?

The snow thickened, two fine curtains of spume driving past him one on either side, cloven by his sturdy body and waving away ahead of him like the ends of a gauze scarf, drawing him forward. Perhaps four times on this ride he had exchanged greetings in passing with other human creatures, and all of them close to home. In such a season only the desperate travel.

It was dark by the time he reached the gatehouse of Bromfield, crossing the footbridge over the little River Onny. His horse had had enough by then, and was blowing frostily, and twitching irritable shoulders and flanks. Cadfael lighted down gladly between the torches in the gateway, and let a lay brother take the bridle. Before him the familiar court opened, straighter than at Shrewsbury, and the shapes of the monastic buildings gilded here and there by the flame of a torch. The church of Saint Mary loomed dark in darkness, large and noble for such a modest foundation.

For Cadfael, his arrival at Bromfield in the brutally cold winter of 1139 to tend Brother Elyas's injuries was the beginning of a search for two stray orphans, a brother and sister, that took him through the wild and inhospitable countryside of southern Shropshire. It was a journey that led to the chilling discovery of the body of a young virgin trapped beneath the ice of a frozen brook; a journey, through forests and woods, hills and valleys, that led to the armed confrontation of her killers on the rocky, wind-swept heights of Titterstone Clee, five miles to the north-east of Ludlow.

It is in this *Sixth Chronicle* that Giles, the son of Aline and Hugh Beringar, is born. Brother Cadfael also discovers that he has a son, born twenty-six years previously in Antioch, a discovery that fills him 'full of wonder and astonishment, all elation and humility'. Suddenly in the midst of winter, eleven days to the Christmas feast, it is a 'time of births, of triumphant begettings, and this year how richly celebrated – the son of the young woman from Worcester, the son of Aline and Hugh, the son of Mariam, the Son of Man.... '

And for Cadfael: 'A son to be proud of! Yes, amen!'

*The Ledwyche Brook*

*Brother Cadfael, Hugh Beringar and his men 'came to the manor of Ledwyche over a slight ridge and emerged from woodland to look down an equally gentle slope toward the Ledwyche brook, into which all the others drained before it flowed on, mile after mile, southward to join the River Teme.'*
        The Virgin in the Ice

'The branches still held up roofs of frozen snow, trailing long icicles where the noon sun had had room to penetrate, and the ground underfoot, deep in leaf-mould and needles, was easy riding. The trees even created a measure of warmth. Clee was a royal forest, but neglected now, as much of England was surely being neglected, left to rot or to be appropriated by opportunist local magnates, while king and empress fought out their battle for the crown. Lonely country, this, and wild, even within ten miles of [Ludlow] castle and town. Assarts were few and far between. The beasts of the chase and the beasts of the warren had it for their own domain, but in such a winter even the deer would starve without some judicious nursing from men. Fodder too precious to be wasted by the farmer might still be put out by the lord to ensure the survival of his game in a bad season.'

*The Virgin in the Ice*

*Clee Forest*

*Titterstone Clee*

*Sunset on the summit of Titterstone Clee*

*'The sunlight had long withdrawn, though the sun itself had still some way to sink, and hung in a dull red ball behind veils of thin grey cloud. The inevitable nocturnal snow should not begin for an hour or two yet. The air was very still and very cold.'*

The Virgin in the Ice

*Clee Hill*

*The Clee Hills, comprising Clee Hill, Titterstone Clee and Brown Clee, are the highest in Shropshire, rising to almost 1,800 feet*

*Church of St Milburgha,*
*Stoke St Milborough*

*The village of Stoke St Milborough shelters in a deep valley on the eastern slopes of the Clee Hills, eleven miles south-west of Bridgnorth and six miles north-east of Ludlow. It is named after St Milburga, Abbess of the monastery of Wenlock towards the end of the seventh century. There is a legend that the saint fell from her horse while being chased by her enemies over the hills and, at the place where she landed, a spring gushed out of the ground. Known as St Milburga's Well, it became a small centre for pilgrimage around which a settlement grew up called God's Stoke. There was a church at Stoke St Milborough in the seventh century and the present church stands on the original Saxon site. In the Middle Ages the church had a number of dependent chapelries, including Heath Chapel.*

*The Clee Hills south of Heath Ho*

*Heath Chapel*

*Standing in lonely isolation in a field, on the western slopes of Brown Clee and just over a mile north-west of Clee St Margaret, is a small chapel – all that is left of the abandoned medieval village of Heath. Remarkably, it has survived unaltered (except for the addition of one nineteenth-century window) since Norman times*

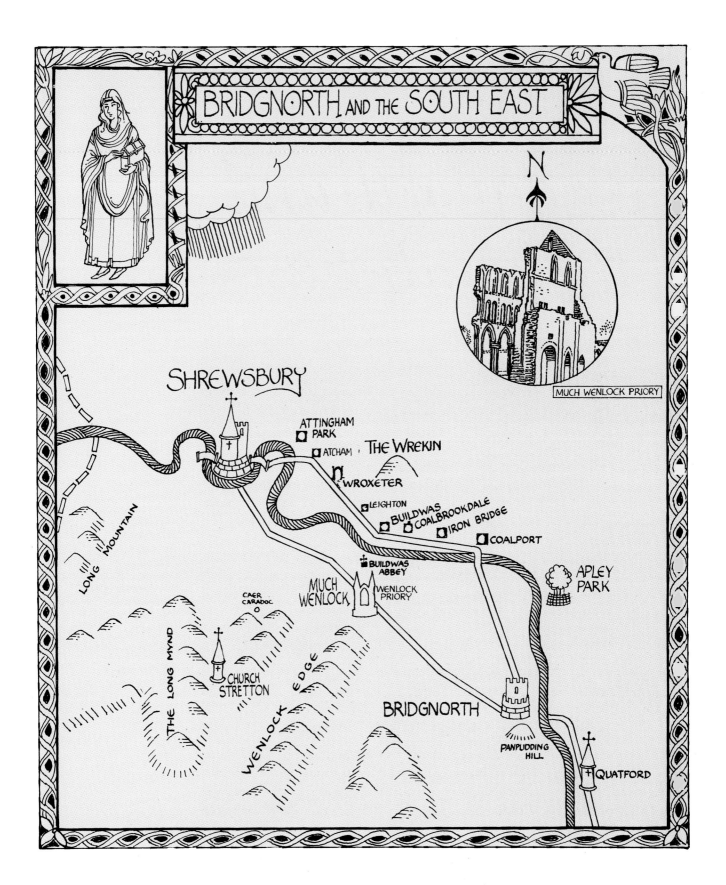

BRIDGNORTH AND THE SOUTH EAST

N

MUCH WENLOCK PRIORY

SHREWSBURY

ATTINGHAM PARK

ATCHAM

THE WREKIN

WROXETER

LEIGHTON

BUILDWAS

COALBROOKDALE

IRON BRIDGE

COALPORT

LONG MOUNTAIN

BUILDWAS ABBEY

MUCH WENLOCK

WENLOCK PRIORY

APLEY PARK

CAER CARADOC

CHURCH STRETTON

THE LONG MYND

WENLOCK EDGE

BRIDGNORTH

PANPUDDING HILL

QUATFORD

# Bridgnorth and the South-East

rom Shrewsbury and the Benedictine Abbey of Saint Peter and Saint Paul, the River Severn meanders in a south-easterly direction towards the hilltop town of Bridgnorth. Although Brigge (as Bridgnorth is called in the *Chronicles*) is eighteen miles from Shrewsbury in a direct line, the course of the river, with its devious twists and turns, almost doubles the distance. Having made a tight loop around Shrewsbury, the river heads north-east, past the castle, doubles back on itself at Uffington, sweeps south past Attingham Park, wriggles like a hooked eel beyond Atcham and suddenly, at Wroxeter, as if exhausted by its strenuous windings, straightens to flow due south.

Wroxeter is mentioned in the *Fourteenth Chronicle of Brother Cadfael (The Hermit of Eyton Forest)* when young Richard Ludel, heir to his late father's estate, is accompanied to Eaton (Eaton Constantine) by Brother Paul, Brother Anselm and Brother Cadfael:

> [They] splashed through the ford at Wroxeter, where centuries back the Romans had crossed the Severn before them. Nothing remained of their sojourn now but a gaunt, broken wall standing russet against the green fields, and a scattering of stones long ago plundered by the villagers for their own building purposes. In the place of what some said had been a city and a fortress there was now a flourishing manor blessed with fat, productive land, and a prosperous church that maintained four canons.

The Roman city of *Viroconium* (Wroxeter) is five miles south-east of Shrewsbury. Although today there are only a few sparse remains, in its prime it was the fourth largest city in Roman Britain and excavations have revealed that it was also the site of a legionary fortress of the first century AD. The Celtic-British tribe of the

*River Severn, near Wroxeter*

*Ford across the River Severn
at Wroxeter*

*The baths, Wroxeter
Roman City*

*The north wall of the
frigidarium (cold room) from
the caldarium (very hot, wet
room) and including the
tepidarium (tepid, wet room).
On each side of the frigidarium
were cold plunge baths. The city
was once the fourth largest in
Britain with defences that
enclosed an area of 180 acres.
There is a small museum on the
site*

Cornovii occupied the Iron Age hill-fort on the summit of the nearby Wrekin, but there is no evidence to suggest that they had a settlement at Wroxeter, which seems to have been founded entirely by the Romans. It was from Wroxeter, situated on the main supply route of Watling Street, and from other military camps in the vicinity of the Wrekin that the legions launched campaigns across the Shropshire border and into Wales (see The Welsh Border, p. 125).

The *Fourteenth Chronicle* continues:

All this stretch of country on the northern side of the river extended before them in rich water-meadows and undulating fields, rising here and there into a gentle hill, and starred with clusters of trees just melting into the first gold of their autumn foliage. The land rose on the skyline into the forested ridge of the Wrekin, a great heaving fleece of woodland that spread downhill to the Severn, and cast a great tress of its dark mane across Ludel land, and into the abbey's woods of Eyton-by-Severn. There was barely a mile between the grange of Eyton, close beside the river, and Richard Ludel's manor house at Eaton. The very names sprang from the same root, though time had prised them apart, and the Norman passion for order and formulation had fixed and ratified the differences.

As they rode nearer, their view of the long hog-back of forest changed and fore-shortened. By the time they reached the manor they were viewing it from its end, and the hill had grown into an abrupt mountain, with a few sheer faces of rock just breaking the dark fell of trees near the summit. The village sat serenely in the meadows, just short of the foothills, the manor within its long stockade raised over an undercroft, and the small church close beside it. Originally it had been a dependent chapel of the church at its neighbour Leighton, downriver by a couple of miles.

Beyond Wroxeter, Eyton-on-Severn, Eaton Constantine and Leighton, the Severn passes to the north of the Savignac Abbey of Our Lady and Saint Chad at

*Church of St Andrew, Wroxeter*

*Although part of the north wall is Anglo-Saxon, most of the Norman Church of St Andrew was built with re-used stone taken from the ruins of the Roman city of Viroconium. In 1155, after Henry II had reinstated his confiscated estates, William Fitz Alan gave the church to Haughmond Abbey and in about 1170–80 the chancel was added. It was longer and wider than the original Saxon nave, which itself was lengthened in the thirteenth century. In the walls of the embattled tower, added in the sixteenth century, are moulded stones from Haughmond Abbey. During the building of the south wall in 1763 the south aisle, which at some time had been added, was removed. The porch is Victorian. Roman columns and capitals were used to build the churchyard gate and the font is fashioned from the base of a Roman pillar. In the south wall of the nave, placed high up and horizontally, is part of an Anglo-Saxon cross-shaft carved with foliage and a dragon.*

*Water-meadows,*
*near Leighton*

 *'Between the forest and the meanderings of the river, downstream from the mill and the fisheries and the few cottages that served them, the open water-meadows extended, and there the light still hung, and a faint ground mist lay veiling the green, and twined like a silver serpent along the river. But along the northern rim the forest continued, halfway to Leighton, and beyond that point the ground rose towards the last low foothills of the Wrekin....'*
The Hermit of Eyton Forest

Buildwas, which was demolished during the Dissolution. It became a Cistercian house when the Savignac and Cistercian Orders were united in 1147. This union was solemnly promulgated at the Council of Rheims in March 1148. Standing in a meadow beside the river, the monastic ruins that remain are impressive. Buildwas is considered one of the finest ruined abbeys in England, surpassed only by Fountains in Yorkshire and Tintern in Gwent. Despite the intervening centuries, the church has managed to survive almost intact except for the roofs and the outer walls of the aisles and the chapel. In addition, parts of the cloister, the chapter-house, the sacristy, the crypt and the parlour still stand. The abbey was founded in 1135 by Roger de Clinton, Bishop of Coventry and Lichfield, who is featured in the *Sixteenth Chronicle (The Heretic's Apprentice)* (see The Journey East to Lichfield, p. 177).

*'[The] new lord of Eaton [Master Richard Ludel] kept to the belt of woodland that stretched westward for half a mile or so above the river, thinning as it went until it was no more than a belt of single oaks spaced out beside the water. Beyond that, emerald water-meadows filled a great bend in the Severn, open and treeless. There he kept inland far enough to have some cover from the few bushes that grew along the headlands of the Leighton fields. Upstream, where he must go, the valley widened into a great green level of flood meadows, with only a few isolated trees on the higher spots, but the northern bank where he rode rose within another mile into the low ridge of Eyton forest, where he could go in thick cover for more than half the distance to Wroxeter.'*

*The Hermit of Eyton Forest*

*River Severn, near Leighton*

*Acton Burnell Castle*

RIGHT *and* BELOW RIGHT:
*The village of Acton Burnell
(simply Acton in the
Chronicles) is situated some
seven miles south-east of
Shrewsbury. The red sandstone
castle (more accurately a fortified
manor house) was built towards
the end of the thirteenth century
by Robert Burnell, Bishop of
Bath and Wells, and Lord
Chancellor under Edward I.
Nearby, in the thirteenth century
Church of St Mary, are the tomb
of Sir Richard Lee and his wife
(1591) a wall memorial to Sir
Humphrey Lee (1632), ancestors
of Richard Henry Lee, one of the
signatories of the American
Declaration of Independence,
and General Robert E. Lee, a
Confederate Leader in the
American Civil War*

*Eyton Forest*

'The morning was clearer of mist than in recent days; there had arisen a steady, drying wind that was crisping the fallen leaves in the forest rides, and colouring in muted gold those that still hung on the trees. The first frost would set the crowns of the forest blazing in russets and browns and flame. Another week or two . . . and there'd be no shelter . . . even the oaks would be half-naked'

*The Hermit of Eyton Forest*

*Looking across cloister to north side of church, Buildwas Abbey*

*After its foundation in 1135, construction of the abbey continued without interruption and by about 1200 the church and the buildings surrounding the cloister were all completed. They remained almost unaltered until the Dissolution. Unlike Shrewsbury Abbey, the cloister at Buildwas lies on the north side of the church*

*Chapter house, Buildwas Abbey*

*River Severn, near Atcham*

'A late boat coming up the Severn from Buildwas next day, and tying up at the [English bridge in Shrewsbury] about nine in the morning, delayed its unloading of a cargo of pottery to ask first that a message be sent to the sheriff, for they had other cargo aboard, taken up out of a cove near Atcham, which would be very much the sheriff's business. Gilbert Prestcote, busy with other matters, sent from the castle his own sergeant, with orders to report first to Hugh Beringar at the abbey.

'The particular cargo the potter had to deliver lay rolled in a length of coarse sail-cloth in the bottom of the boat, and oozed water in a dark stain over the boards. The boatmen unfolded the covering, and displayed to Beringar's view the body of a heavily built man of some fifty to fifty-five years, fleshy, with thinning, grizzled hair and bristly, bluish jowls, his pouchy features sagging doughily in death. Master Thomas of Bristol, stripped of his elaborate capuchon, his handsome gown, his rings and his dignity, as naked as the day he was born.

'"We saw his whiteness bobbing under the bank," said the potter, looking down upon his salvaged man, "and poled in to pick him up, the poor soul. I can show you the place, this side of the shallows and the island at Atcham. We thought best to bring him here, as we would a drowned man. But this one," he said very soberly, "did not drown."'

*Saint Peter's Fair*

Three miles south of Buildwas are the ruins of Wenlock Priory, originally founded towards the end of the seventh century by Merewald, a Mercian king, whose daughter Milburga was the first Abbess. Little is known about the subsequent history of the monastery until after the Norman Conquest, when Wenlock was granted to Earl Roger de Montgomery, who refounded it as a Cluniac priory sometime between 1079 and 1082 (see Shrewsbury Abbey, p. 69).

In the *First Chronicle (A Morbid Taste for Bones)* Prior Robert Pennant's 'campaign to secure the relics and patronage of a powerful saint' for the monastery at Shrewsbury is triggered by events at Wenlock Priory:

> The prior had had it on his mind, in fact, ever since the Cluniac house of Wenlock had rediscovered, with great pride and jubilation, the tomb of their original foundress, Saint Milburga, and installed her bones triumphantly on their altar. An alien priory, only a few miles distant, with its own miracle-working saint, and the great Benedictine house of Shrewsbury as empty of relics as a plundered almsbox! It was more than Prior Robert could stomach. He had been scouring the borderlands for a spare saint now for a year or more, looking hopefully towards Wales, where it was well known that holy men and women had been common as mushrooms in autumn in the past, and as little regarded.

Robert is eventually led to the grave of Saint Winifred in the remote Welsh village of Gwytherin, and from there her bones, sealed inside in a silver-ornamented reliquary, are brought back to Shrewsbury and their 'final resting place on the altar of the abbey church' (see Saint Winifred, p. 85).

*Norman arches of chapter house, Wenlock Priory*

*Lying at the north-eastern tip of Wenlock Edge, the small market town of Much Wenlock was granted borough status in 1468 by Edward IV. There are a number of timber-framed buildings in the town, including the Guildhall, which dates from 1577. The large Church of Holy Trinity dates from the middle of the twelfth century and contains a chapel dedicated to St Milburga. During the Middle Ages the town was dominated by the Cluniac Priory, founded by Roger de Montgomery after the Norman Conquest. The priory church was rebuilt and enlarged in the 1220s by Prior Humbert. When completed it was over 350 feet long. At the close of the fifteenth century great cracks appeared in the vaulting over the high altar, and the church had to be extensively repaired. It was probably at about this time that the Lady Chapel was rebuilt. After the Dissolution, Wenlock Priory was stripped of its valuables, including the lead from the roofs, and its buildings and estates were sold. Although all that remain of the other buildings are ruins, the Prior's house – lavishly rebuilt in about 1500 – survived.*

*South transept of church from near the north porch, Wenlock Priory*

*Ironbridge Gorge*

*River Severn in Ironbridge Gorge*

Downstream from Buildwas the river gathers pace, flowing deep and swift as it rushes between the steep and heavily wooded limestone cliffs of the narrow Severn Gorge and under the world's first cast-iron bridge, erected in 1779. The Iron Bridge was designed by Abraham Darby III, whose grandfather, Abraham Darby I, was the first man successfully to smelt iron using coke instead of the traditional charcoal, which was scarce and, therefore, more expensive. In consequence, the iron industry, no longer restricted by dwindling supplies of charcoal, was able to expand and thereby bring about a revolution in large-scale industrial production that was to sweep throughout the Western world. The pioneering efforts of the Darby family of ironmasters, combined with the local abundance of natural resources, attracted other industries to the district. It is not surprising, therefore, that the four-mile stretch of the Severn, between Coalbrookdale and Coalport, including Ironbridge, has been heralded as 'The Birthplace of the Industrial Revolution'.

Beyond Coalport the river sweeps south, past Apley Park, where there is a large Gothic-style mansion, built of Grinshill stone in 1811. In *The Severn Valley* (published in 1862), J. Randall wrote:

> For the finest view of this splendid park the visitor should ascend its noble terrace, and from Belle Vue look down upon the picture at his feet. The river, like a silver thread, interweaves itself with the splendid carpet in the vale, and the scene which unfolds itself is harmonious and soothing as a hymn. Fat pastures, enclosed by woods, are dotted with cattle, while sprightly deer graze near patches of bright green fern. It is fearful to look down the precipice at your feet, and over the tops of trees, above one of which a hawk is preparing to pounce on its prey. It is sublime to cast the eye over the sylvan slopes and cloud-shadowed sweeps into the distance, where the Wrekin pierces the horizon. It is solemn and impressive to tarry here till evening, till the burning sun has set behind the hill, and the moon is rising to take its place.

Three miles south of Apley Terrace the Severn arrives at Bridgnorth, where it passes under a six-arched stone bridge which links the upper town on the western side of the river to the smaller and lower town on the eastern bank. High Town, as the upper part is called, is situated on a sandstone ridge overlooking the Severn valley with a church at each end. The northern church, dedicated to Saint Leonard, was built in 1860–62; while the southern church, dedicated to Saint Mary Magdalene and designed by Thomas Telford, was begun in 1792. Near the Church of Saint Mary Magdalene are the leaning ruins of Bridgnorth Castle. To the south-west, behind the station of the Severn Valley steam railway, is a large and ancient mound known as Panpudding Hill, which is thought to have been the site of a timber fortification erected by Ethelfleda, the eldest daughter of Alfred the Great, in about 912 as a defence against Danish incursions.

*Bridgnorth Castle*

*During the reign of King Stephen, Bridgnorth Castle was seized by Hugh de Mortimer, who held it until 1155 when it was besieged and taken by Henry II. By the close of the thirteenth century it had declined in importance and was allowed to fall into decay. Today only part of the tower of the Norman keep remains, leaning at a seemingly perilous angle of seventeen degrees from the perpendicular. The castle grounds are now a public park*

'The Danes had reached no further south than Brigge in this shire, but they had left a few of their getting behind when they retreated', states the *Thirteenth Chronicle (The Rose Rent)*. Indeed, the first mention of Bridgnorth in historical records refers to the Danes setting up a camp in about 895 at Cwatbridge, which may have been Bridgnorth, but more probably Quatford a couple of miles downstream.

By 1086, when the Domesday Book was compiled, the Anglo-Saxon castle at Bridgnorth seems to have deteriorated, for it is not mentioned in the survey. There is mention, however, that Roger de Montgomery, Earl of Shrewsbury, had a small 'Borough called Quatford' in which he founded a church dedicated to Saint Mary Magdalene.

Earl Roger's son, Robert de Bellême, became the Third Earl of Shrewsbury in 1098 (see Shrewsbury, p. 53) and three years later he transferred the church and 'Borough' to Bridgnorth. According to the *Ecclesiastical History of England and Normandy* by Ordericus Vitalis, Robert 'built a very strong castle at Brigge, on the River Severn'. Situated on the summit and at the southernmost end of the high sandstone ridge, the fortress was ideally positioned to defend itself against assault, whether from the west or from the east and along the Severn valley.

In 1101 Robert de Bellême, with other Anglo-Norman nobles, conspired to dethrone King Henry I and place the English crown on the head of his elder brother, Robert of Normandy. Henry, however, negotiated a peaceful settlement with his brother and, in the following year, laid siege to Bridgnorth Castle. After three months the castle fell and, with victory almost certain, the King and his army marched north to besiege Earl Robert in his stronghold at Shrewsbury.

Ordericus Vitalis describes the state of the road over Wenlock Edge, through which they had to march:

> This road was for a thousand paces full of holes, and the surface rough with large stones, and so narrow that two men on horseback could scarcely pass each other. It was overshadowed on both sides by a thick wood, in which bowmen were placed in ambush, ready to inflict sudden wounds with hissing bolts and arrows, on the troops on their march. There were more than 60,000 infantry in the expedition; and the king gave orders that they should clear a broad track, by cutting down the wood with axes, so that a road might be formed for his own passage, and a public highway for ever afterwards. The royal command was promptly performed, and vast numbers of men being employed, the wood was felled, and a very broad road levelled through it.

Seeing that he was in no position to win, Robert de Bellême rode south from Shrewsbury, confessed his treason and, according to J.C. Anderson (*Shropshire: its Early History and Antiquities*) 'humbly laid the keys of the town at the king's feet, and sued for mercy'. In consequence he was banished from England and his lands, castles and properties were forfeited to the Crown.

In the *Eleventh Chronicle (An Excellent Mystery)* Hugh Beringar rode south-east to Bridgnorth to ask Walter the cooper's wife, Elfrid, if she knew the whereabouts of her brother Adam Heriet:

> Walter the cooper had a shop in the hilltop town of Brigge, in a narrow alley no great way from the shadow of the castle walls. His booth was a narrow-fronted cave that drove deep within, and backed on an open, well-lit yard smelling of cut timber, and stacked with his finished and half-finished barrels, butts and pails, and the tools and materials of his craft. Over the low wall the ground fell away by steep, grassy terraces to where the Severn coiled, almost as it coiled at Shrewsbury, close about the foot of the town, broad and placid now at low summer water, with sandy shoals breaking its surface, but ready to wake and rage if sudden rains should come.

A number of caves can still be seen in the sandstone cliffs of Bridgnorth and at Cartway (the road leading from High Town to Low Town) there are some which were occupied right up until 1856.

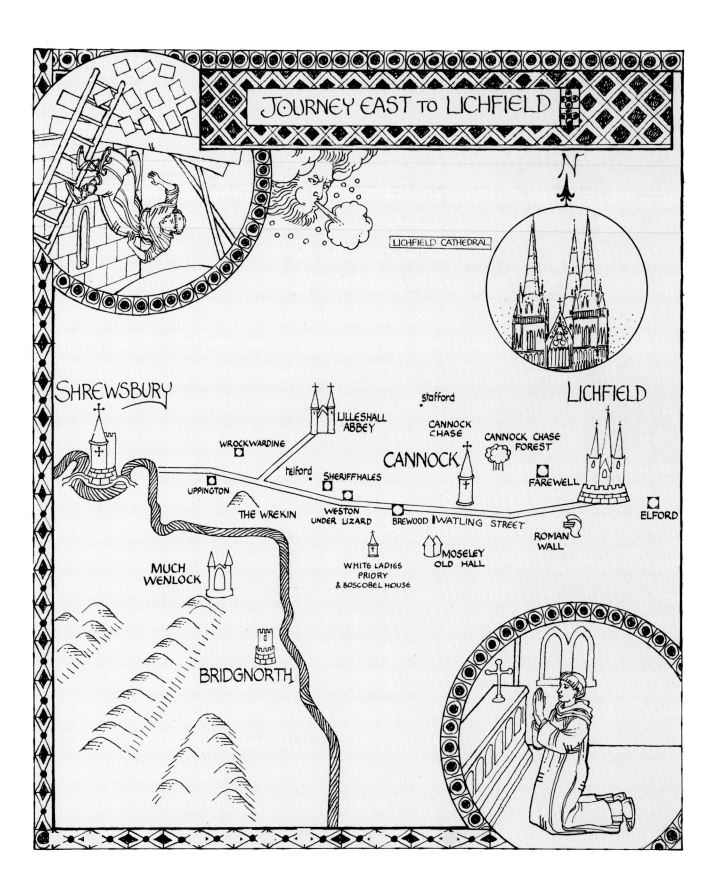

JOURNEY EAST TO LICHFIELD

LICHFIELD CATHEDRAL

SHREWSBURY

LILLESHALL ABBEY

WROCKWARDINE

stafford

CANNOCK CHASE

CANNOCK CHASE FOREST

LICHFIELD

CANNOCK

telford

UPPINGTON

SHERIFFHALES

FAREWELL

THE WREKIN

WESTON UNDER LIZARD

BREWOOD WATLING STREET

ELFORD

ROMAN WALL

WHITE LADIES PRIORY & BOSCOBEL HOUSE

MOSELEY OLD HALL

MUCH WENLOCK

BRIDGNORTH

# The Journey East to Lichfield

I n the spring of 1143 Brother Cadfael set out from Shrews-
bury on a sixteen-mile or so journey to the de Clary manor of
Hales (Sheriffhales), 'towards the eastern edge of the shire'.
The reason for the journey was to accompany Brother
Haluin, who could walk only with the assistance of crutches,
on a penitential pilgrimage to the tomb of Bertrade de Clary.
While on his deathbed, Haluin had confessed to poisoning this young woman,
or, at least, to supplying the poison that had killed her.

The journey, which continues from Hales another twenty-three miles to
Lichfield and a further four to Elford, is related in the *Fifteenth Chronicle of
Brother Cadfael (The Confession of Brother Haluin)*. The events leading up to it are as
follows. After a heavy snowfall in December 1142, the guest-hall roof at the
Benedictine Abbey of Saint Peter and Saint Paul at Shrewsbury began to leak.
'The great weight of snow on the southern roof of the guest-hall had somehow
worked a passage through the lead and filtered in between the slates, perhaps
even caved in a number of them.' An urgent conference was called and it was
decided that repairs should be carried out as 'soon as the long snowfall ceased,
and the skies lifted'. By the time 'a few of the main highways were again
passable, and a few travellers, either foolhardy or having no choice, were
laboriously riding them, Brother Conradin had his scaffolding up, his ladders
securely braced up the slope of the roof, and all hands taking their turn aloft in
the withering cold, cautiously shifting the great burden of snow, to get at the
fractured lead and broken slates'.

Although Brother Haluin had 'a delicate hand with the brushes and pens', he
refused any privilege and took his turn in the biting cold on the roof with the

rest of the brothers. Unfortunately, while wishing to sweep away the snow to uncover some slates, he caused the 'rounded bank of snow to shift'.

> [It] slid down in great folds upon itself, and fell, partly upon the end of the planks and the stack of slates waiting there, partly over the edge and sheer to the ground below. No such avalanche had been intended, but the frozen mass loosed its hold of the steep slates and dropped away in one solid block, to shatter as it struck the scaffolding. Haluin had leaned too far. The ladder slid with the snow that had helped to keep it stable, and he fell rather before than with it, struck the end of the planks a glancing blow, and crashed down without a cry to the frozen channel below. Ladder and snowfall dropped upon the planks and hurled them after him in a great downpour of heavy, sharp-edged slates, slashing into his flesh.

Miraculously, although Haluin's legs were shattered, he managed to survive and, having confessed to a sin 'long past', he vowed to make a journey of expiation. Gradually and painfully he recovered and, although the accident had left him a cripple, by the following spring he was well enough to approach Abbot Radulfus for permission to leave. As the Abbot did not believe Haluin was fit to make the journey alone, he charged Brother Cadfael to accompany him.

> Small choice, thought Cadfael, but not altogether displeased at the instruction, either. There was still, somewhere deep within him, a morsel of the *vagus* who had roamed the world from Wales to Jerusalem and back to Normandy for forty years before committing himself to stability within the cloister, and an expedition sanctioned, even ordered, by authority could be welcomed as blessed, instead of evaded as a temptation.
>
> 'If you so wish, Father,' he said, 'I will.'

That same evening after Vespers, at the altar of Saint Winifred, Brother Haluin recorded his solemn oath:

'"On these most holy relics," he said, with his palm pressed against the drapings that covered the reliquary, "I record my penitential vow: that I will not rest until I have gone on foot to the tomb in which Bertrade de Clary lies, and there passed a night's vigil in prayer for her soul, and again on foot returned here to the place of my due service. And if I fail of this, may I live forsworn and die unforgiven."'

> They set out after Prime, on the fourth morning of March, out at the gate and along the Foregate towards Saint Giles and the highroad due east. The day was cloudy and still, the air chill but not wintry cold. Cadfael viewed the way ahead in his mind, and found it not too intimidating. They would be leaving the western hills behind them, and with every mile eastward the country about them would subside peaceably into a green level. The road was dry, for there had been no recent rain, and the cloud cover above was high and pale, and threatened none, and there was a grassy verge such as could be found only on the king's highways, wide on either side of the track, easy

walking even for a crippled man. The first mile or two might pass without grief, but after that the constant labour would begin to tell. He would have to be the judge of when to call a halt, for Haluin was likely to grit his teeth and press on until he dropped. Somewhere under the Wrekin they would find a hospitable refuge for the night, for there were abbey tenants there among the cottagers, and any hut along the way would willingly give them a place by the fire for a midday rest. Food they had with them in the scrip Cadfael carried.

In the brisk hopefulness of morning, with Haluin's energy and eagerness at their best, they made good speed, and rested at noon very pleasurably with the parish priest at Attingham. But in the afternoon the pace slowed somewhat, and the strain began to tell upon Haluin's hardworking shoulders, aching from the constant weight and endlessly repeated stress, and the cold as evening approached numbed his hands on the grips of his crutches, in spite of their mufflings of woollen cloth. Cadfael called a halt as soon as the light began to fade into the windless March dusk, grey and without distances, and turned aside into the village of Uppington, to beg a bed for the night at the manor.

The next day was less kind, for there was a thin, spasmodic rain that stung at times with sleet, and a colder wind from the north-east, from which the long, green, craggy bulk of the Wrekin gave them no shelter as the road skirted it to the north. But they reached the priory [of Augustinian canons at Wombridge, now a suburb of Telford] before dusk, though Haluin's lips were fast clenched in determination by then, and the skin drawn tight and livid over his cheekbones with exhaustion, and Cadfael was glad to get him into the warmth, and go to work with oiled hands on the sinews of his arms and shoulders, and the thighs that had carried him so bravely all day long.

And the third day, early in the afternoon, they came to the manor of Hales.

*The Church of St Bartholomew, Farewell*

*The tiny hamlet of Farewell is situated some two miles north-west of Lichfield and six miles east of Cannock. A small abbey of Benedictine nuns was founded here in about 1140 by Roger de Clinton, Bishop of Lichfield and Coventry. It declined to a priory in the mid-thirteenth century and was dissolved in 1527, before the general Dissolution. The church was pulled down and rebuilt in the mid-eighteenth century, except for the stone chancel dating from about 1300 once used by the nuns*

*Church of Saint Eata, Atcham*

*The western slopes of the Wrekin*

*The volcanic hog-back of the Wrekin rises dramatically from the flat Shropshire plain. Its summit is 1,335 feet above sea level and from it there is an extensive view embracing more than twelve counties. The Wrekin is rich in legends and folklore and some of the tales try to account for the names of its natural features, for example, Hell Gate, Heaven Gate, the Needle's Eye and the Raven's Bowl*

### The road to Atcham

'The highroad had a broad margin of turf on either side, soft green walking, the veil of cloud had tempered the sun's heat, the meadows were green on either hand, full of flowers and vibrant with insects, and in the bushes and headlands of the fields the birds were loud and full of themselves, shrilling off rivals, their first brood already fledged and trying their wings. Cadfael rolled contentedly along the green verge, the grass stroking silken cool about his ankles. Now if the end came up to the journey, every step of the way would be repaid with double pleasure.

Before him, beyond the level of fields, rose the wooded hogback of the Wrekin, and soon the river reappeared at some distance on his left, to wind nearer as he proceeded, until it was close beside the highway, a gentle, innocent stream between flat grassy banks, incapable of menace to all appearances, though the local people knew better than to trust it. There were cattle in the pastures here, and waterfowl among the fringes of reeds. And soon he could see the square, squat tower of the parish church of Saint Eata [at Atcham] beyond the curve of the Severn, and the low roofs of the village clustered close to it.'

*The Heretic's Apprentice*

*In 1086, at the time of the Norman survey, Recordine or Wrockwardine was held by Earl Roger de Montgomery, the founder of Shrewsbury Abbey. It lies a few miles north of the Wrekin and is thought to derive its name from 'Wrekin Worthen' or the 'village under the Wrekin'. Originally a Saxon foundation, the present Church of St Peter was built in the twelfth century. By the beginning of the following century a new crossing tower, transepts and chancel had been added, and early in the fourteenth century the top of the tower was embattled and the west end rebuilt. The north chapel was constructed in the late fourteenth century and the south chapel in the fifteenth century. The church is a prominent landmark on the flat plain between Shrewsbury and Wellington.*

*Church of St Peter, Wrockwardine*

Brother Cadfael and Brother Haluin entered the manor and asked for an audience with the Lady Adelais de Clary, Bertrade's mother. After Haluin had begged her forgiveness, which was readily given, they departed in search of the church, within which was the de Clary family tomb. To Haluin's consternation, they found that Bertrade was not there and that there had been no burial in the tomb for more than thirty years, 'since the old lord died'.

It was pointed out, however, by the local priest that Hales was ' "not the chief seat of the de Clary honour, for that's Elford, in Staffordshire. The present lord Audemar took his father there for burial, the family has a great vault there. If there are any close kin dead these last years, that's where they'll be. No doubt the lady you speak of was also taken there to lie among her kinsfolk." '

'Haluin seized upon the hope hungrily. "Yes ... yes, it could well be so, it must be so. There I shall find her." '

Refusing the priest's offer of food and a place to rest overnight, Haluin insisted on taking advantage of what little daylight was left to press on with the journey.

'No!' said Cadfael firmly, as soon as they were clear of the churchyard, and passing along the track between the village houses to reach the highroad. 'That you cannot do!'

'I can, I must!' Brother Haluin responded with no less determination. 'Why should I not?'

'Because, in the first place, you do not know how far it is to Elford. As far again as we have come, and half as far after that. And you know very well how hard you have pushed yourself already. And in the second place, because you were given leave to attempt this journey in the belief that it would end here, and we two return from here. And so we should. No, never shake your head at me, you know very well Father Abbot never envisaged more than that, and would never have given you leave for more. We should turn back here.'

*West front of church,
Lilleshall Abbey*

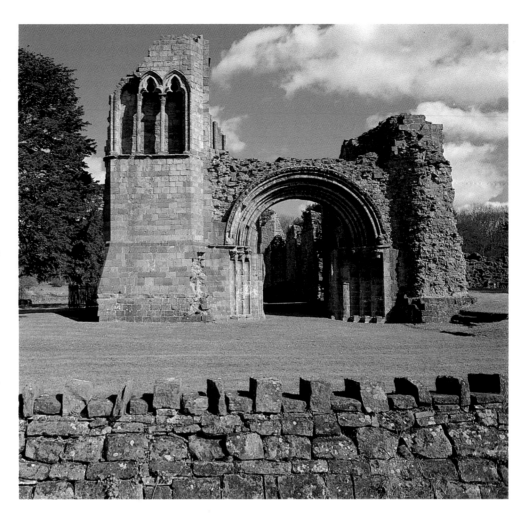

*East processional door and book
locker, Lilleshall Abbey*

*In the fields one mile to the south of the village of Lilleshall, set against a backdrop of woodland, are the ruins of the Augustinian Abbey of St Mary. It was founded in about 1148 by Richard de Belmeis as a monastery of the Arrouasian Order, consisting of a small community of canons which his brother Philip had brought from Dorchester, Oxfordshire, a few years earlier and had established at Tong, near Shifnal. This order was later absorbed by the Augustinians. After its dissolution in 1538, Lilleshall Abbey was granted to William Cavendish, ancestor of the Dukes of Devonshire, who sold it the following year to James Leveson of Wolverhampton. During the Civil War Sir Richard Leveson converted the abbey into a Royalist stronghold and, in consequence, those buildings which managed to survive the Dissolution were badly damaged by the Parliamentarians.*

*Castle Ring Iron Age hill-fort,
Cannock*

*To the east of the town of
Cannock (originally known as
Chenet) are the earthwork
remains of an Iron Age hill-fort
built around 500 BC. Situated
over 750 feet above sea-level, the
fort occupies the highest point of
Cannock Chase and from it
there are extensive views over
the surrounding area. Evidence
of what was probably a medieval
hunting-lodge has been found
in a corner of the nine-acre site*

*Cannock Forest*

*Cannock Chase, part of which
is now a 2,400-acre Country
Park, was once a royal preserve
and its forest was used by
Plantagenet kings for hunting*

'How can I?' Haluin's voice was implacably reasonable, even tranquil. His way was perfectly clear to him, and he was patient with dissent. 'If I turn back, I am forsworn. I have not yet done what I vowed to do; I should go back self-condemned and contemptible. Father Abbot would not wish that, however little either he or I expected so long a penance. He gave me leave until I had accomplished what I swore to do. If he were here to be asked, he would tell me to go on. I said I would not rest until I had gone on foot to the tomb where Bertrade lies buried, and there passed a night in prayer and vigil, and that I have not done.'

It was obvious that no amount of argument would persuade the dogged penitent to turn back to Shrewsbury. Cadfael resigned himself to the fact, saying: '"If your mind's made up, so is mine. Where you go, I go. And since we have barely an hour of daylight left to us, and I fancy you have no wish to seek a bed here in Hales, we had better move gently on, and look for a shelter along the way."'

Before the light failed, they managed to walk a further four miles or so, crossing the border into Staffordshire, and spent the night with 'a solitary cottar and his wife a mile or so beyond the hamlet of Weston' (Weston-under-Lizard). Two miles south of their overnight stop was the small Augustinian Priory of the White Ladies at Brewood, where, in the *Fifth Chronicle (The Leper of Saint Giles)*, Joscelin Lucy intended to ask sanctuary for Iveta de Massard 'until enquiry could be made into her affairs, and a proper provision made for her'.

After a long day in which they travelled a further ten miles directly east along the old Roman road of Watling Street, Cadfael and Haluin went to bed early in 'the hay-loft of a forester's holding in the royal forest of Chenet' (Cannock). The following night they were taken in by the manor of Chenet itself, 'in the king's holding', and the next day saw them in Lichfield,

*Church of St Michael on Greenhill, Lichfield*

> where Cadfael was determined they should halt for another long night's rest, however ardently Haluin might argue for pressing on the remaining few miles to Elford. After a proper sleep in Lichfield Haluin should be in better condition to endure the next night's vigil pledged in Bertrade's memory, and face the beginning of the return journey, during which, God be praised, there need be no haste at all, and no cause to drive himself to the limits of endurance.

Lichfield is about forty miles due east of Shrewsbury and was the ecclesiastical centre of the ancient kingdom of Mercia before the Norman Conquest. The first cathedral church to be erected at Lichfield was consecrated in 700 to enshrine the bones of Saint Chad, Bishop of the Mercians, who died in 672. Bede, in *The Ecclesiastical History of the English Nation*, describes Saint Chad's first shrine (others were built later) as 'a wooden monument, made like a little house, covered, having a hole in the wall, through which those that go thither for devotion usually put in their hand and take out some of the dust, which they put into

*White Ladies' Priory, Brewood*

At the time of the Norman Conquest there was an extensive forest in the area between Telford and Cannock, known as the Royal Forest of Brewood. Located almost in its heart was the White Ladies Priory, a house of Augustinian nuns who were called white ladies because of the colour of their undyed habits. Dedicated to St Leonard, the priory was founded at about the beginning of the twelfth century, but the foundation was small; in 1377 there were nine nuns and, at its dissolution in 1536, there were even fewer. By the seventeenth century the priory was part of a large house belonging to the Roman Catholic Giffards but it was demolished in the following century. A mile to the north-east of the priory is Boscobel House, built by the Giffards as a hunting-lodge in about 1600. It was here, after the Battle of Worcester in 1651, that Charles II hid in an oak to avoid capture by Cromwell's forces. White Ladies Priory and Boscobel House are both open to the public and are administered by English Heritage.

*Lichfield Cathedral*

The present cathedral at Lichfield, dedicated to St Mary and St Chad, was built of red sandstone between 1195 and 1325 and is the only one in England with three spires, known as the Ladies of the Vale. The Lady Chapel was added at the east end in the fourteenth century. During the Civil War the Parliamentarians demolished the central spire and severely damaged the rest of the cathedral. The building was restored during the reign of Charles II, but much rebuilding was again necessary in the late eighteenth century because of decay. One of the treasures of the cathedral, housed within the chapter house, is the priceless Lichfield Gospels, an illuminated manuscript dating from the early eighth century. It came to the cathedral from Wales about a thousand years ago, but where it originated, or who wrote it, remains a mystery.

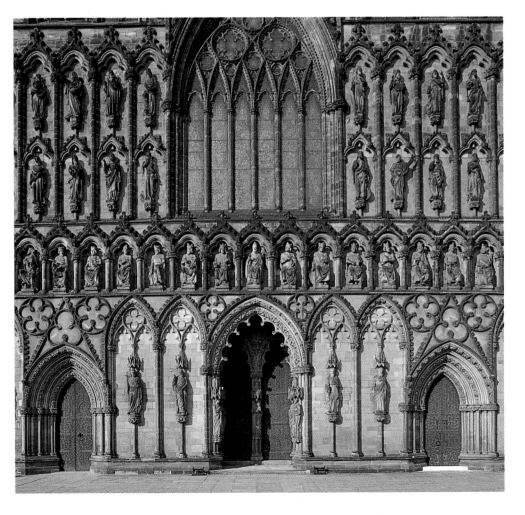

*West front, Lichfield Cathedral*

water and give to sick cattle or men to drink, upon which they are presently eased of their infirmity, and restored to health'.

In 1135 (eight years before Brother Cadfael's and Brother Haluin's journey to Lichfield) work started on replacing the old wooden cathedral with one of stone, built in the Norman style. Bishop Roger de Clinton, who instigated the rebuilding, appears in the *Sixteenth Chronicle (The Heretic's Apprentice)* to judge the charge of heresy brought against Elave, apprentice to William of Lythwood, a wool merchant of Shrewsbury. The Bishop, in whose extensive diocese Shrewsbury Abbey lay, is described as 'a man of good repute, devout and charitable if austere, a founder of religious houses and patron of poor priests'.

According to the *Chronicles*, Roger de Clinton came to the Abbey of Saint Peter and Saint Paul at Shrewsbury in the summer of 1143.

> He had been bishop for fourteen years, and wore his authority as easily and forthrightly as he did his plain riding clothes, and with the same patrician confidence. He was tall, and his erect bearing made him appear taller still. A man austere, competent, and of no pretensions because he needed none, there was something about him, Cadfael thought, of the warrior bishops who were becoming a rare breed these days. His face would have done just as well for a soldier as for a priest, hawk-featured, direct and resolute, with penetrating grey eyes that summed up as rapidly and decisively as they saw.

Although Roger de Clinton was Bishop of Lichfield, one of his 'predecessors in office had transferred the chief seat of his diocese' to Coventry, 'though it was still more often referred to as Lichfield than as Coventry, and both churches considered themselves as having cathedral status'. On its completion in about 1140, the Bishop dedicated the cathedral at Lichfield to Saint Mary and Saint Chad. Roger de Clinton eventually joined the Second Crusade and died at Antioch in April 1148.

From Lichfield Brother Cadfael and Brother Haluin continued their long and arduous journey east to Elford in search of the final resting-place of Bertrade de Clary. They found the de Clary tomb in the little Norman church, on the east bank of the River Tame, and Haluin spent a long, cold 'night of prayer' beside it and 'redeemed his vow'. In mid-afternoon of the next day, having accomplished their task, the two Benedictine monks from Shrewsbury left Elford for the long walk home.

The journey back, however, is far from uneventful and 'leads to shocking discoveries: of young lovers thwarted; of deceit and betrayal; of bitter revenge ... and of murder'. And once more, Brother Cadfael had to unravel the twisted threads to discover the truth.

*Church of St Chad, Lichfield*

*The church (dedicated to Saint Chad, Bishop of the Mercians in the seventh century) stands at the north-eastern end of Stowe Pool. It was built beside an ancient spring, where the saint is said to have founded a monastery*

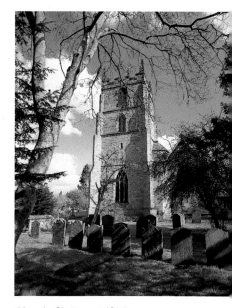

*Church of St Peter, Elford*

*The church contains an impressive collection of tombs and monuments of the late lords of the manor*

# Postscript

More than nine hundred years have passed since Earl Roger founded the Abbey of Saint Peter and Saint Paul at Shrewsbury. Since that distant time, the town, abbey and surrounding area have changed almost beyond recognition. Although the loop of the Severn has restricted growth within the town centre itself, Shrewsbury has expanded outwards in almost every direction. The open countryside, mentioned in the *Chronicles* as lying between the Benedictine monastery and the hospital of Saint Giles, has disappeared, now swallowed by the eastern suburbs.

Since its construction in the mid-nineteenth century, the railway, with its extensive yards and sidings, has prevented any major building development to the south of the abbey. However, there are now proposals to redevelop the entire Reabrook valley – the area of land stretching from the Reabrook round-about in the south-east to the Abbey Foregate in the north. One element of these proposals, known as Abbey 2000, is to reunite the abbey church with the rest of its original site, some areas of which, between 1985 and 1988, have been excavated by the Birmingham University Field Archaeology Unit. Vibration from the heavy traffic using the busy main road running through the original abbey site is damaging the church and, within the plans, it is envisaged that there will be a traffic-free precinct around the historic building. Abbey 2000's intention is to make the northern end of the site into a major international tourist centre, not only catering for the needs of the increasing number of people coming to visit the historic abbey but also providing cultural and educational facilities.

The cost of preservation, however, is horrendous and the Abbey Restoration Project – dedicated to the upkeep of the Abbey of Saint Peter and Saint Paul – urgently requires funds. Although much more needs to be done, the *Chronicles of Brother Cadfael* have helped to focus attention on the historic value and plight of the building. Now, however improbable it may seem, the future survival of the ancient abbey may partly rest in the broad hands of a stocky Welshman, a soldier turned monk, who 'sprang to life suddenly and unexpectedly' in 1977 – perhaps just when he was needed most!

For further details of Abbey 2000 and the Shrewsbury Abbey Restoration Project, or even to make a contribution to the enormous cost of preservation, please contact:

Shrewsbury Abbey
Restoration Project
Shrewsbury Abbey
Abbey Foregate
Shrewsbury
SY2 6BS
Telephone: (0743) 232723

# Visitor Information

## Properties Open to the Public

## THE NATIONAL TRUST

**Attingham Park**
Shrewsbury
Shropshire, SY4 4TP
Telephone (House
enquiries): (074 377) 203

Park and grounds open daily throughout
the year except Christmas Day. House
open from Easter to the end of
September, Saturday to Wednesday;
open weekends in October.

**Carding Mill Valley and Long Mynd**
Chalet Pavilion
Carding Mill Valley
Church Stretton
Shropshire, SY6 6JG
Telephone: (0694) 722631

Moorland open daily throughout the
year. Café, shop and information centre
open from Easter to the end of
September; open weekends in October.

**Chirk Castle**
Chirk
Clwyd, LL14 5AF
Telephone: (0691) 777701

Open daily from Easter to the end of
September, except Monday and Saturday
(open Bank Holiday Monday); open
weekends in October.

**Letocetum**
Wall (Baths and Museum)
Watling Street
Wall
nr Lichfield
Staffordshire, WS14 0AW
Telephone: (0543) 480768

Open daily from Easter to the end of
September; open daily except Monday
from October to Easter.

**Moseley Old Hall**
Moseley Old Hall Lane
Fordhouses
Wolverhampton
Staffordshire, WV10 7HY
Telephone: (0902) 782808

Open from mid-March to the end of
October Wednesday, Saturday and
Sunday; open Tuesday in July and
August; open Bank Holiday Monday.

**Powis Castle**
Welshpool
Powys, SY21 8RF
Telephone: (0938) 554336

Open daily from Easter to the end of
June except Monday and Tuesday; open
July and August daily except Monday;
open September and October daily
except Monday and Tuesday; open Bank
Holiday Monday.

# ENGLISH HERITAGE

**Boscobel House**
Brewood
Shropshire, ST19 9AR
Telephone: (0902) 850244

Open daily throughout the year.

**Buildwas Abbey**
Ironbridge
Telford
Shropshire, TF8 7BW
Telephone: (0952) 453274

Open daily throughout the year.

**Haughmond Abbey**
Upton Magna
Uffington
Shrewsbury
Shropshire, SY4 4RW
Telephone: (0743) 77661

Open daily throughout the year.

**Lilleshall Abbey**
Abbey Road
Lilleshall
nr Oakengates
Shropshire, TF10 9HW
Telephone: (0952) 604431

Open Summer season.

**Stokesay Castle**
Craven Arms
Shropshire, SY7 9AH
Telephone: (0588) 672544

Open daily from March to the end of
October except Tuesday.

**Wenlock Priory**
Much Wenlock
Shropshire, TF13 0HS
Telephone: (0952) 727466

Open daily throughout the year.

**Wolvesey Castle**
Old Bishop's Palace
Off College Street
Winchester
Hampshire
Telephone: (0962) 54766
Open daily from Easter
to end September.

**Wroxeter Roman City**
Wroxeter
Shropshire, SY5 6PH
Telephone: (0743) 75330

Open daily throughout the year.

# GAZETTEER

## ACTON SCOTT

**Acton Scott Working Farm Museum**
Wenlock Lodge
Acton Scott
nr Church Stretton
Shropshire, SY6 6QN
Telephone: (069 46) 306/307

Open daily from April to October.

## HOLYWELL

**St Winefride's Well**
New Road
Holywell
Clwyd, CH8 7PN
Telephone: (0352) 713054

Open daily throughout the year; services daily from Whit Sunday to September and by arrangement.

## IRONBRIDGE

**The Ironbridge Gorge Museum**
(Visitor Information Service)
Ironbridge
Telford
Shropshire, TF8 7AW
Telephone: (0952 45) 3522 (weekdays)
2751/2166 (weekends)

Open daily throughout the year except Christmas Eve and Christmas Day; some small sites closed from November to February.

## LINCOLN

**Lincoln Castle**
Castle Hill
Lincoln, LN1 3AA
Telephone: (0522) 511068

Open daily throughout the year except Sundays between October and April. Also closed Christmas Day, Boxing Day and New Year's Day.

## LUDLOW

**Ludlow Castle**
Castle Square
Ludlow
Shropshire
Telephone: (0584) 873947

Open daily from February to December.

## SHREWSBURY

**Bear Steps**
St Alkmond's Square
Shrewsbury
Shropshire, SY1 1UH
Telephone: (0743) 56511

Open daily except Sundays.

**Clive House Museum**
College Hill
Shrewsbury
Shropshire, SY1 1LT
Telephone: (0743) 54811

Open weekdays except Monday mornings.

**Rowley's House Museum**
Barker Street
Shrewsbury
Shropshire, SY1 1QT
Telephone: (0743) 61196

Open daily except Sundays.

**Saint Mary's Church**
Saint Mary's Square
Shrewsbury
Shropshire

Although the church is now in the care of the Redundant Churches Fund it remains open to visitors for part of each weekday and occasional weekends.

**Shrewsbury Abbey**
Abbey Foregate
Shrewsbury
Shropshire, SY2 6BS
Telephone: (0743) 248859 (vicarage)
232723 (abbey office)

Open daily throughout the year.

**Shrewsbury Castle**
[including the Shropshire Regimental Museum]
Shrewsbury
Shropshire, SY1 2AT
Telephone: (0743) 58516

Open daily throughout the year, except Sundays between October and Easter.

WESTON-UNDER-LIZARD

**Weston Park**
Weston-under-Lizard
nr Shifnal
Shropshire, TF11 8LE
Telephone: (095 276) 385/207

Open Easter to September. Weekends only in April, daily in August, and daily except Monday and Friday, May to July and September.

YOCKLETON

**Shropshire Country World**
Yockleton
Shrewsbury, Shropshire, SY5 9PU
Telephone: (074 384) 217

Open daily from
Easter to end October.

## *Tourist Information Offices and Other Useful Addresses*

## THE NATIONAL TRUST

MERCIA REGION

**Regional Public Affairs Department**
The National Trust
Mercia Regional Office
Attingham Park
Shrewsbury
Shropshire, SY4 4TP
Telephone: (074 377) 343

NORTH WALES REGION

**Regional Public Affairs Department**
The National Trust
North Wales Regional Office
Trinity Square
Llandudno
Gwynedd, LL30 2DE
Telephone: (0492) 860123

## ENGLISH HERITAGE

**Head Office**
English Heritage
25 Savile Row
London, W1X 2BT
Telephone: (01) 973 3000

**Midland Regional Information Office**
English Heritage
Finchfield House
Castlecroft Road
Wolverhampton, WV38 8BU
Telephone: (0902) 765105

## GAZETTEER

BRIDGNORTH

**Tourist Information Office**
The Library
Listley Street
Bridgnorth
Shropshire, WV16 4AW
Telephone: (07462) 763358/763257

**Severn Valley Railway**
(northern terminus at Bridgnorth)
The Railway Station
Bewdley
Worcestershire, DY12 1BG
Telephone: (0299) 403816

CHURCH STRETTON

**Shropshire Hills Information Centre**
Church Street
Church Stretton
Shropshire, SY6 6DQ
Telephone: (0694) 723133

Open only in summer season.

IRONBRIDGE

**Tourist Information Centre**
5 The Wharfage
Ironbridge
Telford
Shropshire, TF8 7AW
Telephone: (095 245) 2166

LICHFIELD

**Tourist Information Centre**
Donegal House
Bore Street
Lichfield
Staffordshire, WS13 6NE
Telephone: (0543) 252109

LUDLOW

**Tourist Information Centre**
Castle Street
Ludlow
Shropshire, SY8 1AS
Telephone: (0584) 875053

Open only in summer season.

MUCH WENLOCK

**Tourist Information Centre**
The Guildhall
Much Wenlock
Shropshire
Telephone: (0952) 727679

Open only in summer season.

OSWESTRY

**Tourist Information Centre**
The Library
Arthur Street
Oswestry
Shropshire, SY11 1JN
Telephone: (0691) 662753

**Tourist Information Centre**
Mile End Service Area
Oswestry
Shropshire, SY11 4JA
Telephone: (0691) 662488

SHREWSBURY

**Tourist Information Centre**
The Square
Shrewsbury
Shropshire, SY1 1LH
Telephone: (0743) 50761

**Shropshire Wildlife Trust**
Old St George's School
New Street
Shrewsbury
Shropshire, SY3 8JP
Telephone: (0743) 241691

WELSHPOOL

**Tourist Information Office**
Vicarage Gardens Car Park
Welshpool
Powys, SY21 7DD
Telephone: (0938) 552043

**Welshpool & Llanfair Light Railway**
The Station
Llanfair Caereinion
Welshpool
Powys, SY21 0SF
Telephone: (0938) 810441

WHITCHURCH

**Tourist Information Office**
The Civic Centre
High Street
Whitchurch
Shropshire, SY13 1AX
Telephone: (0948) 4577

# Select Bibliography

**Select references used by Ellis Peters for _The Chronicles of Brother Cadfael_:**

Anderson, John Corbet, _Shropshire: Its Early History and Antiquities_, Willis and Sotheran, 1864

Chibnall, Marjorie, _The World of Orderic Vitalis_, Oxford, 1984

_Culpeper's Illustrated Herbal_, Foulsham, 1983 (NB In addition, Ellis Peters has another version of _Culpeper's Herbal_, 'dilapidated copy published by Joseph Smith, High Holborn, too early to bear a date, but certainly earlier than 1838 when my great-grandfather wrote his name and date of ownership in it'.)

Gimpel, Jean, _The Medieval Machine_, Gollancz, London, 1977

Hamel, Christopher de, _A History of Illuminated Manuscripts_, Phaidon, 1986

Harvey, John, _Mediaeval Gardens_, Batsford, London, 1981

Henken, Elissa, _Traditions of the Welsh Saints_, Brewer, 1987

Hunt, Tony, _Plant Names of Medieval England_, Brewer, 1989

Knowles, David, _The Monastic Order in England_, Cambridge University Press, 1976

Lloyd, Sir J. E., _A History of Wales: From the Earliest Times to the Edwardian Conquest_, Longmans, Green and Co., 1954

Owen, H. and Blakeway, J. B., _A History of Shrewsbury_ (2 vols.), Harding, Lepard and Co., 1825

Pain, Nesta, _Empress Matilda_, Weidenfeld and Nicolson, London, 1978

Poole, Austin Lane, _The Oxford History of England: From Domesday to Magna Carta_ (2nd edition), Oxford University Press, 1975

Potter, K. R., ed. and translator, _Gesta Stephani_, Oxford Medieval Texts, 1976

Rees, Una, ed. and translator, _The Cartulary of Shrewsbury Abbey_, National Library of Wales, Aberystwyth, 1975

Savage, Anne, translator and collator, _The Anglo-Saxon Chronicles_, Heinemann, London, 1982

Steane, John M., _The Archaeology of Medieval England and Wales_, Croom Helm, 1985

_The 'Brut Y Tywysogion' (The Chronicles of the Princes)_ (3 differing versions), University of Wales Press, 1952–5

**Additional select references used by Robin Whiteman for *Cadfael Country*:**

Barber, W. T., *Exploring the Marches and Borderlands of Wales*, Alan Sutton, Gloucester, 1984

Baugh, G. C. and Cox, D. C., *Monastic Shropshire*, Shropshire Libraries, Shrewsbury, 1982

Bede, *A History of the English Church and People*, (Sherley-Price, Leo, translator), Penguin Books, Harmondsworth, 1955

*The Benedictines in Britain*, The British Library, London, 1980

Blackwall, Anthony, *Historic Bridges of Shropshire*, Shropshire Libraries, Shrewsbury, 1985

Boston, Noel, *The Story of Lilleshall Abbey*, 1934

Bottomly, Frank, *The Explorer's Guide to the Abbeys, Monasteries and Churches of Great Britain*, Avenel Books, New York, 1981

Dickinson, J. C., *Monastic Life in Medieval England*, Adam and Charles Black, London, 1961

Dodd, A. H., *Life in Wales*, Batsford, London, 1972 (republished as *A Short History of Wales*)

Evans, Kathleen M., *A Book of Welsh Saints*, Church in Wales Provincial Council for Education, Penarth, 1959

Forrest, H. E., *The Old Churches of Shrewsbury*, Wilding, Shrewsbury, 1920

Fraser, Maxwell, *Welsh Border Country*, Batsford, London, 1972

Garner, Lawrence, *Shropshire* (Shire County Guide: 7), Shire, Aylesbury, Buckinghamshire, London, 1985

Green, Howard, *The Battlefields of Britain and Ireland*, Constable, London, 1973

Hughes, Cledwyn, *The Northern Marches*, Hale, London, 1953

Jackson, Michael, *Castles of Shropshire*, Shropshire Libraries, Shrewsbury, 1988

James, M. R., *Abbeys*, The Great Western Railway, 1925

Mee, Arthur, *Shropshire* (The King's England series), Hodder and Stoughton, London, 1939 (revised 1968)

Moran, Madge, *Bear Steps*, Shrewsbury Civic Society, Shrewsbury, 1982

Owen, H., *Some Account of the Ancient and Present State of Shrewsbury*, Sandford, Shrewsbury, 1808 (republished by Morten, Manchester, 1972)

Pargeter, Edith, *The Heaven Tree Trilogy*, Heinemann, London, 1960–63

Parry, David, *The Rule of Saint Benedict*, Darton, Longman and Todd, London, 1984

Peake, Harold, *Historical Guide to Ellesmere* (local guide), Roberts, Ellesmere, 1897

Pevsner, Nikolaus, *Shropshire* (The Buildings of England series), Penguin Books, Harmondsworth, 1958

Platt, Colin, *The Abbeys and Priories of Medieval England*, Secker and Warburg, London, 1984

Platt, Colin, *The English Medieval Town*, Secker and Warburg, London, 1976

Priestley, E. J., *An Illustrated History of Shrewsbury*, Shrewsbury and Atcham Borough Council, Shrewsbury, 1982

Pryce-Jones, John, *Historic Oswestry*, Shropshire Libraries, Shrewsbury, 1982

Randall, J., *The Severn Valley*, James S. Virtue, London, 1862

Reeves, Marjorie, *The Medieval Monastery*, Longman, London, 1958

Roderick, A. J., ed., *Wales through the Ages: Vol. 1*, Davies, Llandybie, 1959

Rowley, Trevor, *The Landscape of the Welsh Marches*, Michael Joseph, London, 1986

Salter, Mike, *The Castles and Moated Mansions of Shropshire*, Folly Publications, Wolverhampton, 1988

Salter, Mike, *The Old Parish Churches of Shropshire*, Folly Publications, Wolverhampton, 1988

Saulles, Mary de, *The Book of Shrewsbury*, Barracuda, Buckingham, 1986

Scott-Davies, A. and Sears, R. S., *Shuts and Passages of Shrewsbury*, Shropshire Libraries, Shrewsbury, 1986

*Shropshire* (county guide), The British Publishing Company, Gloucester, 1988

*The Shropshire Village Book* (compiled by the Shropshire Federation of Women's Institutes), Countryside Books, Newbury, 1988

Stenton, Doris Mary, *English Society in the Early Middle Ages* (The Penguin History of England series), Penguin Books, Harmondsworth, 1951

Thorn, Frank and Caroline, eds., *Domesday Book: Shropshire*, Phillimore, Chichester, 1986

Thurston, Herbert J. and Attwater, Donald, eds., *Butler's Lives of the Saints* (4 vols.), Burns and Oates, London, 1926–38

Trinder, Barrie, *A History of Shropshire*, Phillimore, Chichester, 1983

Waite, Vincent, *Shropshire Hill Country*, Dent, London, 1970

Walcott, Mackenzie E. C., *The Four Minsters Round the Wrekin*, Simpkin, Marshall and Co., 1877

Whitelock, Dorothy, *The Beginnings of English Society* (The Penguin History of England series), Penguin Books, Harmondsworth, 1952

Whitelock, Dorothy, ed., *English Historical Documents: Volume I, c. 500–1042*, Eyre Methuen, London, 1979

## The Chronicles of Brother Cadfael by Ellis Peters
*(published by Headline in hardback and Futura in paperback):*

*A Morbid Taste for Bones,* 1977
*One Corpse Too Many,* 1979
*Monk's-Hood,* 1980
*Saint Peter's Fair,* 1981
*The Leper of Saint Giles,* 1981
*The Virgin in the Ice,* 1982
*The Sanctuary Sparrow,* 1983
*The Devil's Novice,* 1983
*Dead Man's Ransom,* 1984
*The Pilgrim of Hate,* 1984
*An Excellent Mystery,* 1985
*The Raven in the Foregate,* 1986
*The Rose Rent,* 1986
*The Hermit of Eyton Forest,* 1987
*The Confession of Brother Haluin,* 1988
*The Heretic's Apprentice,* 1989
*The Potter's Field,* 1989

*A Rare Benedictine,* Headline, London, 1988

# Index